Strengthening Workforce Resilience in U.S. Space Command

KAYLA M. WILLIAMS, MAREK N. POSARD, RYAN HABERMAN, SAMANTHA MATTHEWS, Hilary Reininger, SAMANTHA RYAN

Prepared for the U.S. Space Command
Approved for public release; distribution is unlimited.

RAND NATIONAL DEFENSE RESEARCH INSTITUTE

For more information on this publication, visit **www.rand.org/t/RRA2566-1**.

About RAND

RAND is a research organization that develops solutions to public policy challenges to help make communities throughout the world safer and more secure, healthier and more prosperous. RAND is nonprofit, nonpartisan, and committed to the public interest. To learn more about RAND, visit www.rand.org.

Research Integrity

Our mission to help improve policy and decisionmaking through research and analysis is enabled through our core values of quality and objectivity and our unwavering commitment to the highest level of integrity and ethical behavior. To help ensure our research and analysis are rigorous, objective, and nonpartisan, we subject our research publications to a robust and exacting quality-assurance process; avoid both the appearance and reality of financial and other conflicts of interest through staff training, project screening, and a policy of mandatory disclosure; and pursue transparency in our research engagements through our commitment to the open publication of our research findings and recommendations, disclosure of the source of funding of published research, and policies to ensure intellectual independence. For more information, visit www.rand.org/about/research-integrity.

RAND's publications do not necessarily reflect the opinions of its research clients and sponsors.

Published by the RAND Corporation, Santa Monica, Calif.
© 2024 RAND Corporation
RAND® is a registered trademark.

Library of Congress Cataloging-in-Publication Data is available for this publication.
ISBN: 978-1-9774-1294-2

Cover: Joshua Armstrong/U.S. Air Force.

About This Report

U.S. Space Command (USSPACECOM) was reestablished as a combatant command in 2019 and has a diverse workforce. Its main goals are to achieve full operational capabilities and to maintain space superiority. To ensure this command's success, it is important to enhance the resilience of its personnel. In this report, we offer best practices to enhance resilience by preventing harmful individual behaviors that reduce resiliency, identify some challenges and barriers to resilience program implementation, and propose recommendations to address these challenges and barriers in the future.

The research reported here was completed in January 2024 and underwent security review with the sponsor and the Defense Office of Prepublication and Security Review before public release.

RAND National Security Research Division

This research was sponsored by USSPACECOM and conducted within the Personnel, Readiness, and Health Program of the RAND National Security Research Division (NSRD), which operates the National Defense Research Institute (NDRI), a federally funded research and development program sponsored by the Office of the Secretary of Defense, the Joint Staff, the Unified Combatant Commands, the Navy, the Marine Corps, the defense agencies, and the defense intelligence enterprise.

For more information on the RAND Personnel, Readiness, and Health Program, see www.rand.org/nsrd/prh or contact the director (contact information is provided on the webpage).

Acknowledgments

We thank our sponsor, USSPACECOM, for supporting this work. Furthermore, we thank USSPACECOM's resilience program manager, Lisa Anderson; equal opportunity coordinator, Augustin Andrade; and sexual assault prevention and response program manager, Marcia Marshall, for their support throughout this research. We are grateful to Lauren Skrabala for improving the prose of this report and to Kirsten Keller and Katherine Kuzminski for their thoughtful reviews of earlier drafts of this report.

Summary

U.S. Space Command (USSPACECOM) was reestablished as a combatant command (CCMD) in 2019 and has a diverse workforce whose goals include achieving full operational capability and maintaining U.S. space superiority. This CCMD's success will require a strategy to enhance and sustain the resilience of its personnel. In this report, we offer best practices for building workforce resilience by preventing harmful individual behaviors that reduce resiliency, identify some challenges and barriers to resilience program implementation, and propose recommendations to address these challenges and barriers in the future.

Issue

A key task for the commander of USSPACECOM is to prepare this CCMD's personnel to compete and win, which includes achieving full operational capability and sustaining a warfighting culture that can adapt to an evolving strategic environment. USSPACECOM personnel are a key resource to achieve this objective. Ensuring that personnel are resilient to the various changes that they confront in their lives—and the strategic environment in which USSPACECOM operates—is a key factor that will enable U.S. space superiority.

Approach

USSPACECOM asked RAND to identify best practices for enhancing resilience, organize these practices using a simple framework, and conduct workshops with selected command personnel to understand their concerns surrounding resilience. These workshops' primary focus was to identify approaches to mitigate various harmful behaviors, specifically discrimination, sexual assault and harassment, hostile work environment, and self-directed harm and suicide.

We adapted a social-ecological framework for resilience that organizes relevant factors by levels of analysis—namely, individuals, their interpersonal relationships, their organizations, and the broader culture of these organizations. Next, we examined how the U.S. Department of Defense (DoD) and the military components approach resilience broadly and reviewed the literature on preventing and responding to these harmful behaviors to capture various approaches for enhancing resilience in military contexts. Finally, we designed and hosted a series of workshops with USSPACECOM personnel to inform our assessment of resilience-related challenges, responsibilities, barriers, and solutions.

Key Findings

- USSPACECOM is a reestablished CCMD with a growing workforce whose composition is diverse, having similar percentages of civilian employees, contractors, and service members from across the military services. To succeed, USSPACECOM will need a strategy to enhance and sustain the resilience of its personnel.
- There are numerous DoD and service-level policies and programs dedicated to preventing and responding to harmful behaviors, such as discrimination, sexual assault and harassment, hostile work environment, and self-directed harm and suicide. However, there are often different tracking mechanisms and resources for service members, civilian employees, and contractors.
- In our literature review, the common themes to prevent and respond to harmful behaviors were improving access to services and reporting channels, enhancing leadership communication and climate, targeting high-risk units, and engaging personnel through skills-focused training.
- Our workshops showed that the concerns about resilience in USSPACECOM focused on personnel issues, cohesion within the command, and leadership. However, because USSPACECOM is a reestablished CCMD, there is a perception of disjointedness among levels of the organization regarding who is supposed to report to whom or from whom to seek support, both within and outside the command.

Recommendations

Using the insights from literature review and workshops, we recommend that USSPACE-COM consider several approaches to enhancing its personnel's resilience.

1. USSPACECOM should streamline, target, and formalize communications about various resilience-building efforts to different classes of personnel within this CCMD.
2. USSPACECOM's contracting officer should consider including language in professional service contracts to clarify what types of resilience-related resources, team building, training, and professional recognition are available to civilian contractors.
3. USSPACECOM should continue to invest in developing a one-stop shop for strengthening resilience at USSPACECOM that connects service members, civil servants, and civilian contractors to all available resources across the entire DoD enterprise.
4. USSPACECOM's resilience-building program personnel should develop interactive, engaging, and targeted training that meets the unique needs of its workforce.

Contents

Figures and Tables

Figures

Tables

CHAPTER 1

Project Objectives and U.S. Space Command Workforce Context

The resilience of personnel is a critical part of workforce readiness and effectiveness, especially for the U.S. Department of Defense (DoD). For example, DoD has increasingly invested in efforts to enhance force resilience since introducing the Total Force Fitness (TFF) framework in 2009 (Meadows et al., 2019). DoD has defined *resilience* as the "ability to anticipate, prepare for, and adapt to changing conditions and withstand, respond to, and recover rapidly from disruptions" (DoD, Office of the Under Secretary of Defense for Acquisition and Sustainment, 2021, p. 2). There are other definitions in the U.S. military context. For example, the U.S. Air Force defines *resilience* as the "ability to withstand, recover, and grow in the face of stressors and changing demands" (Air Force Instruction 90-5001, 2023, p. 4).

The American Psychological Association offers a useful starting point for defining workplace resilience for U.S. Space Command (USSPACECOM) as "the process and outcome of successfully adapting to difficult or challenging life experiences," because this organization develops policies and resources to support the unique needs of its personnel (American Psychological Association, undated). In this context, resilience is determined by both the challenging experiences one faces and one's ability to adapt to those challenges (e.g., emotionally, culturally). Enhancing resilience involves both reducing the prevalence of challenging experiences and promoting an individual's ability to adapt when confronted with stressors and changing demands.

USSPACECOM approached RAND to better understand the evidence for various programs designed to enhance resilience and address resilience-related challenges. In consultation with the sponsor, we narrowed the focus of this research effort to opportunities for USSPACECOM to reduce the prevalence of specific harmful behaviors that can arise in the workplace: discrimination, sexual assault and harassment, hostile work environment, and self-directed harm and suicide. The assumption is that these harmful individual behaviors could adversely affect the resilience of USSPACECOM personnel.

DoD has long recognized harmful behaviors that undermine unit and team cohesion, reduce readiness and resiliency, and diminish the effectiveness of the force. Such behaviors include gender and racial discrimination, bullying, harassment, and sexual assault and other forms of violence (Harrell and Miller, 1997; Keller et al., 2015; Morral et al., 2021; Szayna et al., 2015). These behaviors are often interrelated. For example, researchers have noted that aggression, gender and sex discrimination, sexual harassment, and sexual assault intersect or exist "as part of a continuum" (RAND Corporation, 2022, p. 2; Larsen, Nye, and Fitzgerald, 2019).

Harmful activities directed at the self, such as substance use, self-harm, and suicide, also degrade force readiness and are linked to workforce challenges (Hourani et al., 2018; Kim et al., 2021; Kim, Kim, and Park, 2019; Klemmer et al., 2021). For example, there is a strong association between bullying and the victim's alcohol use (Kim et al., 2021). Hazing and sexual harassment are significantly associated with mental health concerns and suicidal behaviors (Campbell-Sills et al., 2023; Griffith, 2019). However, improved unit cohesion is associated with reduced harmful behaviors under certain conditions (Anderson et al., 2019). Therefore, strategies to prevent and address these challenges have the potential to help USSPACECOM build the resiliency of its force, which would ideally enhance its ability to accomplish the commander's goal to "outthink and outmaneuver our adversaries, operate with our allies and partners, and when necessary, win through space combat power" (Dickinson, 2022, p. 3). We note that Gen Stephen N. Whiting took over as commander of USSPACECOM in January 2024, after the writing of this report (USSPACECOM, 2024).

History of USSPACECOM

USSPACECOM was reestablished as a U.S. combatant command (CCMD) in 2019, and as of 2024, its headquarters was located at Peterson Space Force Base in Colorado Springs, Colorado (see Appendix A for background on CCMDs). The decision on where to locate a CCMD's headquarters influences which designated Combatant Command Support Agent (CCSA) is responsible for the administrative and logistical support of the CCMD's headquarters, including various resilience-related programs (DoD Directive 5100.03, 2017).

On April 15, 2019, the Secretary of the Air Force was designated the interim CCSA for USSPACECOM (DoD, Office of the Inspector General, 2022). Most resiliency services for USSPACECOM are located at Schriever Space Force Base and Peterson Space Force Base in Colorado Springs, Colorado (USSPACECOM, undated-b). However, not all USSPACECOM offices are located at these two U.S. Space Force installations; some are located at civilian office parks. The decision about where USSPACECOM's headquarters would be located has been contentious, after a planned relocation to Alabama from 2021 was canceled in July 2023, but as of 2024, the CCMD has remained at its original, interim location at Peterson Space Force Base, with the Department of the Air Force as the command's executive agent.

Given that USSPACECOM is a reestablished CCMD, we include some comparisons of workforce resilience practices of USSPACECOM with other CCMDs throughout this report. Information on other CCMDs was identified from literature reviews, CCMD websites, and open web searches for resources, services, or literature on resilience practices that are available from other CCMDs. Information on USSPACECOM was obtained in similar ways and by conducting workshops with current USSPACECOM personnel groups (see Chapter 3).

USSPACECOM's Workforce

As of April 2023, USSPACECOM had an estimated 1,753 assigned personnel, including those from the component commands, representing dramatic growth from just 123 personnel four years earlier (USSPACECOM, 2023a). Figure 1.1 shows the projected growth of headquarters staff from 2023 to 2025. USSPACECOM expected to grow its staff by more than 10 percent from January 2023 to July 2025.

No single category of personnel constitutes the majority of USSPACECOM, as shown in Figure 1.2. Roughly equal percentages of the workforce are contractors (34 percent), federal civilians (32 percent), and military service members (34 percent, combining enlisted and officer personnel). Among service members, a greater portion are officers (23 percent of all staff) than enlisted (11 percent of all staff). By contrast, enlisted personnel are roughly 82 percent of all active-duty personnel, and officers are only 18 percent (Military OneSource, undated). By 2025, however, nearly two-thirds of headquarters personnel will be federal civilian employees, and the number of contractors is expected to shrink (USSPACECOM, 2023a).

USSPACECOM draws its military workforce from all the service branches. Figure 1.3 shows that 29 percent of USSPACECOM service members are from the U.S. Space Force, 28 percent from the U.S. Army, 20 percent from the U.S. Air Force, 18 percent from the U.S.

FIGURE 1.1

Projected Change in USSPACECOM Headquarters Staff, 2023–2025

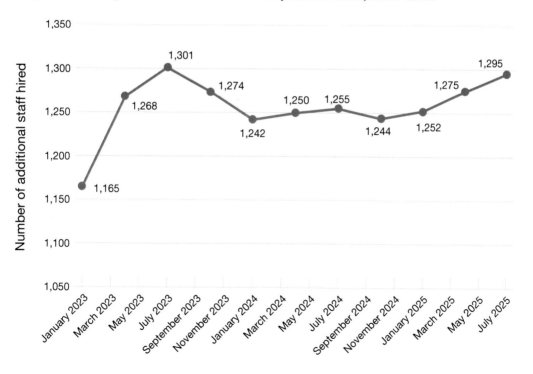

SOURCE: Features data from USSPACECOM, 2023a.

FIGURE 1.2

USSPACECOM Workforce Composition, by Category

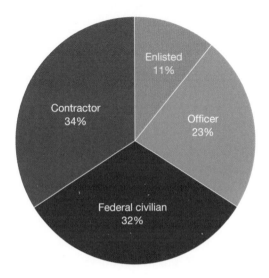

SOURCE: Features data from USSPACECOM, 2023a.

FIGURE 1.3

USSPACECOM Workforce Composition, by Service Branch

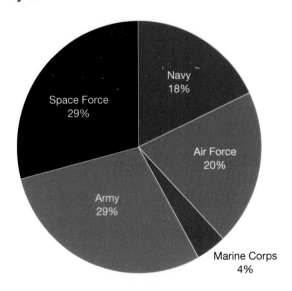

SOURCE: Features data from USSPACECOM, 2023a.

Navy, and 4 percent from the U.S. Marine Corps (USSPACECOM, 2023a). In the broader active-duty force, about 35 percent of service members are in the Army, 26 percent in the Navy, 13 percent in the Marine Corps, 26 percent in the Air Force, and less than 1 percent in the Space Force. Accordingly, USSPACECOM, which is the most recently established CCMD, is drawing disproportionately heavily from the U.S. Space Force, which is the newest military component (Military OneSource, undated).

Demographically, the USSPACECOM workforce is predominantly White and male. One in five personnel at USSPACECOM identifies as a woman and one in four identifies as a person of color (USSPACECOM, 2023a). The average age of USSPACECOM's civilian employees is 46.2 years, while the average age of its military members is 41.0 years. By contrast, the average age of the total active-duty force is 28.5 years, and the average age of officers in the active-duty population is 34.3 years (Military OneSource, undated).

A Social-Ecological Framework for Resilience

We defined workplace resilience in the context of USSPACECOM as the capacity for individuals to adapt to difficult life events that they confront. Figure 1.4 shows a social-ecological framework to organize how individuals may adapt to these experiences, which aligns with DoD's Prevention Plan of Action, a DoD-wide strategy to prevent harm and abuse in the force

FIGURE 1.4
Social-Ecological Framework for Resilience

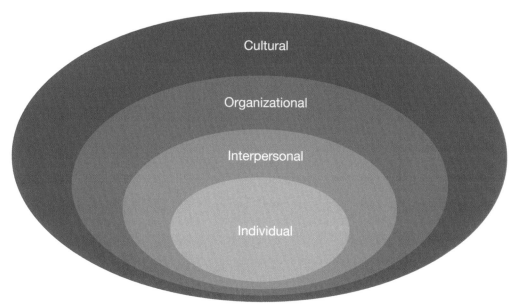

SOURCE: Adapted from Centers for Disease Control and Prevention, 2022.

(DoD, Office of the Under Secretary of Defense for Personnel and Readiness, 2022). Specifically, this framework shows four distinct levels of analysis.

The first level is made up of *individual* service members and civilian employees, including their knowledge, skills, and abilities. Next, an *interpersonal* level includes the family members, friends, and coworkers whom individuals seek out for support when they confront challenging experiences. These relationships tend to be informal.

Third, the *organizational* level involves the places where people occupy formal roles and responsibilities, such as officer versus enlisted, or manager versus subordinate, in formal organizations, such as a CCMD. Some examples of relationships at this level include USSPACECOM leadership, the command's Resilience Program, or the Judge Advocate General's Corps. Finally, *cultural* is the highest level of analysis in Figure 1.4, defined as historically determined beliefs shared by a group of people within the same organization who have common historical experiences (Schooler, 1994). Cultural beliefs can include service- or military-specific traditions, as well as broader societal norms.

Relevance for USSPACECOM

USSPACECOM's Human Capital Strategy 2023 details three strategic goals: (1) attract and retain talent; (2) build and sustain a culture of professionalism, respect, and excellence; and (3) invest in people to achieve success (USSPACECOM, 2023a).

Although all three of these goals relate to resilience, the second goal has the clearest link to the goal of ensuring that personnel adapt to difficult or challenging experiences in their lives while at USSPACECOM. This goal includes several objectives that are related to maintaining a safe workplace that is free from sexual harassment, assault, or any form of discrimination. It includes accepting others; promoting help-seeking and help-offering; and taking time to celebrate accomplishments, recognize achievements, and promote cultural awareness. The third goal also includes an objective to improve employee engagement and personal well-being.

USSPACECOM has pursued several lines of effort geared toward increasing workforce resilience. For example, it held Resilience Focus Week in August 2023, which gave joint directorate teams an opportunity to participate in team activities or training to enhance workforce resilience (USSPACECOM, 2023b). Suggested activities fell into three broad categories:

1. team-building activities, both on- and off-site, to encourage interaction outside the working environment through games
2. wellness activities, such as presentations from health services representatives and group health promotion classes
3. training opportunities through the Air Force Employee Assistance Program (EAP), Military and Family Life Counseling Services, or Military OneSource.

Resilience Focus Week also featured human relations training, such as a leadership and communication seminar; an equal opportunity course; and a diversity, equity, inclusion, and accessibility training session (USSPACECOM, 2023b).

As a reestablished CCMD with a growing workforce whose composition is diverse, USSPACECOM will need a strategy to enhance and sustain the resilience of its personnel to succeed. This report offers best practices for building workforce resilience, identifies challenges and barriers to resilience, and includes recommendations to address these challenges and barriers in the future.

USSPACECOM asked RAND to identify best practices for enhancing resilience, organize these practices using a simple framework, and conduct workshops with selected USSPACECOM personnel to understand their concerns surrounding resilience. The primary focus of these workshops was to identify approaches to mitigate various harmful behaviors, including suicide and self-directed harm, sexual assault and sexual harassment, and equal employment opportunity violations.

Research Approach

This research focuses on ways to mitigate specific types of harmful behaviors (i.e., discrimination, sexual assault and sexual harassment, hostile work environment, and self-directed harm or suicide) as they relate to the resilience of personnel. We follow a two-step approach. First, we reviewed the literature on resiliency in the military, harmful behaviors in the military, and relevant policies about these topics. This literature review is summarized in Chapter 2. Second, we developed and administered a workshop protocol to a sample of SPACECOM personnel to identify salient themes related to problematic behaviors and resiliency. This workshop protocol and summaries of the participants' discussions are included in Chapter 3. As we discuss in this report, a salient theme from our limited sample of participants is organizational issues related to resiliency within USSPACECOM. These results provide a starting point for USSPACECOM to begin prioritizing various efforts to further enhance workforce resilience across this CCMD.

Finally, in Chapter 4, we highlight relevant lessons and best practices from the literature on resilience, focusing on DoD policies, various harmful behaviors that can erode resilience, and the training and education that can improve resilience. We supplement this review with input from our workshop participants, including USSPACECOM service members and civilian employees who shared their resilience-related concerns. We find that participants were less concerned about harmful behaviors than organizational issues. Specifically, several participants noted a lack of cohesion among service members, civilian employees, and civilian contractors, as well as a lack of a sense of identity within USSPACECOM. We conclude this report by proposing recommendations for USSPACECOM to streamline, scale, and invest in its resilience programs as it grows its workforce and matures in its mission and capabilities.

CHAPTER 2

Lessons and Best Practices from the Literature

We gathered information on current and future threats to USSPACECOM workforce resilience by reviewing DoD policy documents, academic research, and prior RAND reports on harmful behaviors. Our literature review method is outlined in Appendix B. As an entry point to this research, we provide an overview of relevant DoD policies and then discuss the harmful individual behaviors of discrimination, sexual assault and harassment, hostile work environment, and self-directed harm and suicide; the relevant DoD policies on these behaviors; and some best practices to prevent and respond to these behaviors. We conclude this chapter with evidence-based programs to address these harmful behaviors and a preliminary assessment of their applicability to USSPACECOM.

Legislation, Regulations, and Policies

DoD policies on preventing harmful behaviors address several key areas, including mental health, sexual harassment and assault, equal opportunity, and discrimination. They are laid out in Department of Defense instructions (DoDIs) at the Office of the Secretary of Defense (OSD) level and instructions and directives at the Joint Chiefs of Staff level, as well as regulations and instruction policy documents at the service levels and below. While regulations at the OSD level and chairman of the Joint Chiefs of Staff level are typically the highest level of DoD authority, some are mandated at the congressional level. For instance, in addition to seeking information and reports through active correspondence and reporting requirements, Congress requires that DoD respond to and address several harmful behaviors that affect resilience through Title 10 of the U.S. Code, the National Defense Authorization Act, and other authorities. Table 2.1 lists the various laws and regulations that DoD must respond to or address.

Office of the Secretary of Defense Policies

The Office of the Under Secretary of Defense for Personnel and Readiness (OUSD[P&R]) is responsible for most policies and regulations on these topics at the DoD level. In addition to this office, the chairman of the Joint Chiefs of Staff also leads DoD-wide policy for the ser-

TABLE 2.1

U.S. Laws and Regulations Related to Harmful Behaviors in DoD

Category	Relevant Laws or Regulations
Discrimination	Code of Federal Regulations, Title 29, Chapter XIV, Equal Employment Opportunity Commission
	U.S. Code, Title 10, Section 481, Racial and Ethnic Issues; Gender Issues: Surveys
Sexual harassment or assault	Code of Federal Regulations, Title 32, Section 105.9, Commander and Management Procedures
	U.S. Code, Title 10, Section 481a, Workplace and Gender Relations Issues: Surveys of Department of Defense Civilian Employees
	U.S. Code, Title 10, Chapter 753, United States Military Academy; Section 7461, Policy on Sexual Harassment and Sexual Violence
	U.S. Code, Title 10, Chapter 953, United States Air Force Academy, Section 9461, Policy on Sexual Harassment and Sexual Violence
	U.S. Code, Title 10, Section 1561, Complaints of Sexual Harassment: Investigation by Commanding Officers
	U.S. Code, Title 10, Section 1562a, Complaints of Retaliation by Victims of Sexual Assault or Sexual Harassment and Related Persons: Tracking by Department of Defense
	U.S. Code, Title 10, Section 1565b, Victims of Sexual Assault: Access to Legal Assistance and Services of Sexual Assault Response Coordinators and Sexual Assault Victim Advocates
Suicide prevention	U.S. Code, Title 10, Section 10219, Suicide Prevention and Resilience Program
Mental health	U.S. Code, Title 10, Section 1074n, Annual Mental Health Assessments for Members of the Armed Forces
	U.S. Code, Title 10, Section 1090b, Commanding Officer and Supervisor Referrals of Members for Mental Health Evaluations

vices through the TFF framework. This instruction "establishes TFF as a key component to the DoD's Force Health Protection Program" (Chairman of the Joint Chiefs of Staff Instruction 3405.01, 2013, p. 1). The TFF framework is relevant to workforce resilience because it "provides the DoD with the capability to understand, assess, and maintain the full spectrum of components affecting Service member readiness and their ability to meet mission requirements" (Defense Health Agency, 2020, slide 2). The TFF program establishes enterprise-level governance of service policies and activities in eight domains of fitness: social, physical, financial, ideological and spiritual, medical and dental preventative care, environmental, nutritional, and psychological.

In 2021, Secretary of Defense Lloyd Austin established the 90-day Independent Review Commission (IRC) on Sexual Assault in the Military to address sexual assault and harassment as "persistent and corrosive problems across the Total Force" (DoD, 2021, Appendix G, p. 1). He ultimately accepted all its recommendations, including the establishment of a dedicated primary prevention workforce (Austin, 2021). DoDI 6400.09 (2020), *DoD Policy on Integrated Primary Prevention of Self-Directed Harm and Prohibited Abuse or Harm*, establishes the policies and responsibilities to mitigate not only sexual harassment and assault but also self-directed harm and other forms of abusive and harmful acts because of their shared risk and protective factors. Integrated primary prevention should focus on the individual, interpersonal, and organizational levels of the social-ecological model, with the goal of fostering healthy behaviors and life skills across career cycles (DoDI 6400.09, 2020, p. 15). Prevention personnel at the command or installation level will identify, adapt, implement, and evaluate research-based prevention programs; these personnel will also consult and collaborate with leaders to optimize access and usage of resources related to prevention efforts (DoDI 6400.09, 2020, p. 12). Military leaders at the command and installation levels are charged to do the same, as well as to encourage a culture of help-seeking and take actions to foster a command climate of dignity, respect, inclusion, and connectedness.

Service Component Policies

In alignment with the OUSD(P&R)'s Office of Force Resiliency and the chairman's TFF framework, each service component maintains a resilience program for its workforce. These programs promote health and resiliency in the eight domains of health, as outlined in the TFF program. The Air Force maintains the Integrated Resilience or Comprehensive Airman Fitness (CAF) program; the Army has the Ready and Resilient (R2) program; and the Navy and Marine Corps use the Expanded Operational Stress Control (E-OSC) program. Table 2.2 outlines the specific goals for each of these programs.

DoD Civilian Policies

In general, military law does not apply to civilian employees. For example, DoD civilian employees are covered by the Civil Rights Act of 1964 and the "standard legal definitions of *racial harassment* and *discrimination* derived from the Civil Rights Act, [whereas] uniformed personnel, both active and reserve, are not" (Matthews et al., 2021, pp. 11–12, emphasis in original). Military Equal Opportunity (MEO) and civilian Equal Employment Opportunity (EEO) are also separate programs with separate reporting mechanisms. In general, monitoring and reporting harmful behaviors among civilians is not required in the same way it is for service members (Bur, 2021), except for sexual assault, sexual harassment, and gender discrimination due to a congressional mandate. Nevertheless, some policies developed and managed by the OUSD(P&R), such as those related to Sexual Assault Prevention and Response (SAPR), apply not only to military personnel but also to DoD civilian employees (DoD, Sexual Assault Prevention and Response Office [SAPRO], undated). The OUSD(P&R)'s Office for Diversity, Equity, and Inclusion, which oversees MEO, also has some EEO responsibilities (DoD, Office for Diversity, Equity, and Inclusion, undated). A key distinction between civilian employees and service members is the types of resources and benefits available to prevent and respond to harmful behaviors.

TABLE 2.2

Service Component Workforce Resilience Programs

Service	Program	Goal
Department of the Air Force (including the Space Force)	Integrated Resilience or Comprehensive Airman Fitness (CAF)	The goal of CAF is to help airmen, Air Force civilians, and their family members become more resilient and better-equipped to deal with the rigors of military life across four domains: mental, physical, social, and spiritual.
Army	Ready and Resilient (R2)	R2 provides training and resources to the Army family to enhance resilience and optimize performance. R2 reinforces the Army's values, beliefs, and attitudes, and educates members of the Army team about the importance of building connections, taking care of one another, and being there to support fellow soldiers.
Department of the Navy (including the Marine Corps)	Expanded Operational Stress Control (E-OSC)	The expanded version of the E-OSC program, which is part of the 21st Century Sailor Office's (OPNAV N17) Behavior Development and Performance Branch (OPNAV N171), will leverage command representatives and deckplate leaders to provide more-accessible, collaborative resources and real-time assessments of unit culture to promote healthy command climates and mitigate risks.
DoD	Total Force Fitness (TFF)	TFF is a framework for building and maintaining health, readiness, and performance in DoD. Health, wellness, and resilience are treated as a holistic concept in which optimal performance requires a connection among mind, body, spirit, and family or social relationships.

SOURCES: Adapted from Joint Base San Antonio, undated, and U.S. Department of the Air Force Integrated Resilience, undated.

NOTE: These programs are available to uniformed service members and government civilians only.

DoD Contractor Policies

Similar to civilians, contractors are often subject to different rules, follow different reporting channels, and have access to different resources, apart from the EEO laws by which contractor and subcontractor agencies must abide under Executive Order 11246 (1965). Federal agencies are responsible for protecting employees from harmful behaviors, such as harassment, assault, and discrimination, from anyone in the workplace. For example, under the EEOC law from the Code of Federal Regulations, Title 29, Part 1604.11, agencies may be responsible for sexual harassment by "non-employees," such as contractors. Federal agencies must also provide contractors, and any others present in the workplace, with the basic information about policies (e.g., non-tolerance of sexual harassment and discrimination) and standards of conduct (e.g., expectations for behavior). In the next section, we focus on the specific types of harmful behaviors and training, education, and relevant programs to addresses these behaviors.

Types of Harmful Behaviors

In this section, we review some of the literature on the four specific harmful behaviors of interest to USSPACECOM: discrimination, self-harm or suicide, sexual assault and sexual harassment, and hostile work environment. For each type of harmful behavior, we searched peer-reviewed academic literature via PubMed, PsycINFO, and Embase, as well as RAND reports, Google Scholar, and bibliographies of research in our samples. Because separate reports could be written on each of these harmful behaviors, we selected and highlighted literature that was most relevant to resilience in general and resiliency as it specifically relates to USSPACECOM at the time of writing this report. Our literature review method is presented in Appendix B.

Discrimination

Although rates of discrimination among civilians and contractors are not collected or reported in a standardized way, the 2017 Workplace and Equal Opportunity Survey of Active Duty Members found that nearly one in five active-duty members (or about 18 percent) "indicated experiencing racial/ethnic harassment and or discrimination in the 12 months prior to taking the survey" (DoD, Office of People Analytics, 2019, p. 14). This DoD report, along with other similar ones focusing on national guard and reserve components, was mandated by Congress because of discrimination rates across DoD.

DoD policy on MEO and discrimination is established by DoDI 1350.02 (2022), *DoD Military Equal Opportunity Program*. MEO offices are located at the service level, not at the CCMDs, except for USSPACECOM, which has the only full-time MEO coordinator at the CCMD level dedicated to meet discrimination issues in its workforce (USSPACECOM, undated-a). However, DoDI 1350.02 (2022), which establishes MEO offices, makes no mention of contractors coming under its protection or purview. This suggests that the range of resilience services for the USSPACECOM workforce is limited for contractors, who make up a large proportion of its workforce.

Best Practices for Preventing and Responding to Discrimination

Our review of academic and technical literature shows key evidence for preventing and responding to discrimination. During trainings, the instructions should emphasize the full range of discriminatory behavior, including but not limited to discrimination related to race, gender, gender expression, sexual orientation, religion, and use of parental leave (Bridges, Wulff, and Bamberry, 2023; Calkins et al., 2022; Farris et al., 2020; Hall et al., 2019; Law and Harris, 2019). Prevention resources should be targeted to those units that are high-risk, and commanders should be aware of known problems within their command (Calkins et al., 2022). Other prevention strategies aim to challenge peer norms and to enhance peer constraints, or social disapproval, and opposition to harmful behaviors (Matthews and Farris, 2022).

Leadership climate is central in predicting racial and ethnic harassment and discrimination, as well as other forms of discrimination; therefore, the leadership's communication of its commitment to a discrimination-free workplace is essential (Calkins et al., 2022; Daniel et al., 2022; Farris et al., 2020; Marquis et al., 2017; O'Keefe, Hing, and Catano, 2023). Studies have found that leaders affect the climate of an organization, which in turn affects the behavior of service members (Marquis et al., 2017; O'Keefe, Hing, and Catano, 2023).

Leadership plays a key role in communicating policies, and leaders are also essential to supporting those who come forward and report harmful behaviors. Those who experienced positive actions after reporting harmful behaviors felt decreased distress, which led to increased retention (Daniel et al., 2022). Leadership should demonstrate accountability and transparency, establish consistency in responding to victims, and build trust in the process of reporting and responding to allegations (Matthews and Farris, 2022).

Sexual Assault and Harassment

Sexual assault and harassment are critical areas that the services have been seeking to address through policy changes and to better understand through survey data. The Workplace and Gender Relations Survey of Military Members—Active Component conducted by the Office of People Analytics in 2021 found that "an estimated 8.4% of women and 1.5% of men in the active component experienced unwanted sexual contact in the year prior to the survey," while an estimated 28.6 percent of women and 6.5 percent of men experienced sexual harassment in 2021 (DoD, Office of People Analytics, 2023, pp. v, 11). The Office of People Analytics also administers a congressionally mandated biennial survey that analyzes trends in DoD civilian employee workplace gender relations. The 2018 report found "overall, an estimated 5.9 percent of DoD civilian employees (an estimated 9.4 percent of women and 3.7 percent of men) experienced *sexual harassment* in the 12 months prior to the survey" (DoD, Office of People Analytics, 2018, p. 3, emphasis in original). This report also found "an estimated 0.3 percent of civilian employees (an estimated 0.6 percent of women and 0.2 percent of men) experienced *work-related sexual assault* in the 12 months prior to the survey," defining *work-related* as when the alleged offender was "someone from work" (DoD, Office of People Analytics, 2018, p. 3, emphasis in original). Importantly, of those who experienced sexual assault or harassment, a minority (an estimated 9 percent to 41 percent for civilian women and an estimated 5 percent to 37 percent for civilian men, depending on the violation) reported it to leadership or filed an EEO complaint,[1] underscoring the need for leadership to communicate the importance of reporting (DoD, Office of People Analytics, 2018).

There are several OSD-level policies and regulations pertaining to sexual assault and harassment. A key regulation in this area is DoD Directive 6495.01 (2021), *Sexual Assault Prevention and Response (SAPR) Program*. This regulation implements DoD policy related to sexual assault prevention among service members and DoD civilians, while also assigning

---

[1] Civilian EEO programs and reporting channels are separate from the MEO programs described above.

responsibilities for the SAPR program. USSPACECOM's Human Capital Strategy provides military and civilian definitions for *harassment*. The civilian definition states that harassment is "behavior that is unwelcome or offensive to a reasonable person and that creates conditions that interfere with work performance or creates an intimidating, hostile, or offensive work environment," whereas the military definition characterizes harassment as "behavior that is unwelcome or offensive to a reasonable person, whether oral, written, or physical, that creates an intimidating, hostile, or offensive environment" (USSPACECOM, 2023a, p. 31). USSPACECOM is the only CCMD with a full-time in-house SAPR program manager (USSPACECOM, undated-c).

Even with these laws, the policies regarding sexual assault and harassment response are less comprehensive for contractors most of the time. For example, all contractors are eligible to receive the support of a victim advocate or sexual assault response coordinator, but the specific policy indicates that the full range of SAPR services are not available to contractors unless "authorized to accompany the Armed Forces in a contingency operation outside of the continental United States" (DoD, SAPRO, undated). There may be state laws governing sexual harassment training that pertain to contractors, but these laws do not mandate any kind of support or response for victims.

Best Practices for Preventing and Responding to Sexual Assault and Harassment

Evidence in academic literature and technical reports indicates key prevention activities. Leadership should identify units with above or below average numbers of cases and should clearly communicate policies and consequences (Gedney et al., 2018). Imposing sanctions for low-level unprofessional behavior can help prevent future escalation and assault, and training should focus on the development of skills, not only knowledge or awareness (Acosta, Chinman, and Shearer, 2021). Training recommendations in the literature consist of incorporating interactive content in trainings and including information on sexual minorities and ways for members to protect themselves (Gedney et al., 2018; Matthews et al., 2018).

Leadership should address key barriers to reporting, which include fear of retaliation and negative perceptions from coworkers or leaders, misunderstandings of what constitutes assault, and logistical issues. Recommendations in the literature include providing multiple confidential reporting channels, tracking and linking claims, and evaluating managers by how they handled claims. For example, echoing DoD's *Retaliation Prevention and Response Strategy: Regarding Sexual Assault and Harassment Reports* (2016), RAND researchers have advocated for "bold actions" (Acosta, Chinman, and Shearer, 2021, p. 9) to create "a culture intolerant of retaliation" and to "hold supervisors and leaders appropriately accountable for preventing, detecting, and addressing retaliatory behavior" (DoD, 2016, pp. 13, 23).

Improving access to resources requires addressing the key barriers to care, such as stigma, coworker or leader perceptions, and logistical factors. Leaders play a central role in supporting those who come forward and should be educated on how to connect victims to services.

Some best practices include hiring staff and allocating sufficient funding toward these efforts, while also continually evaluating and monitoring the progress of these efforts (Calkins et al., 2022; Centers for Disease Control and Prevention, National Center for Injury Prevention and Control, 2016; Farris et al., 2021).

Hostile Work Environment

The hostile work environment, or workplace violence, policy for the military falls under some of the same overarching policies as sexual assault and harassment but includes additional forms of harassment, such as DoDI 1020.03 (2018), *Harassment Prevention and Response in the Armed Forces*. Other types of harassment include discriminatory harassment, hazing, bullying, and stalking. DoDI 1020.03 (2018, p. 3) notes that DoD aims to prevent this behavior because it "jeopardizes combat readiness and mission accomplishment, weakens trust within the ranks, and erodes unit cohesion." Furthermore, DoDI 1438.06 (2020, p. 1), *DoD Workplace Violence Prevention and Response Policy*, establishes the workplace violence prevention and response policy for DoD civilian personnel that covers threats, harassment, intimidation, and "other disruptive behavior."

Best Practices for Preventing and Responding to Hostile Work Environment

Best practices in hostile work environment prevention include screening out high-risk recruits, targeting training to high-risk individuals and units, and conducting trainings that not only build knowledge but also develop skills in identifying and reporting hostile behaviors (Matthews and Farris, 2022). It is also important for leadership to openly communicate hazing policies and to clearly define hazing (Keller et al., 2015; Matthews, Hall, and Lim, 2015). DoD defines *hazing* as causing another to "suffer or be exposed to any activity which is cruel, abusive, humiliating, oppressive, demeaning, or harmful" (Paparo, 2021). In addition to defining hazing, it is helpful to provide example scenarios, so that service members can build a common understanding of hazing activities (Miller et al., 2019). Hazing prevention should also target peer norms and emphasize bystander interventions (Matthews and Farris, 2022; Waldron, 2012).

The literature shows that leadership should build trust in the reporting process; provide confidential, anonymous, and third-party reporting channels; track and link claims; and ensure that no retaliation or negative effects on reporters' careers occur (Keller et al., 2015; Matthews and Farris, 2022; Matthews, Hall, and Lim, 2015). Indeed, one study found that those who reported bullying indicated most commonly that their reason for reporting was that they "trusted that [their] supervisor or commander would address the issue" (U.S. Department of the Air Force, 2021, p. viii). It should be noted that rank is associated with willingness to report, and thus, different reporting mechanisms may be needed for different ranks (Low et al., 2024).

Furthermore, research finds that leadership should be consistent in responding to victims (Matthews and Farris, 2022). One study highlighted the "central role of organizational factors in bullying" and noted that "[p]olicies to prevent bullying must address the culture of organizations" (Feijó et al., 2019, p. 1). Leaders should create a culture of accountability and hold managers accountable for responding to claims (Keller et al., 2015; Matthews, Hall, and Lim, 2015). Other recommendations in the literature include hiring or assigning an individual or office to oversee these efforts, prioritizing this work in strategic plans, and continually evaluating and monitoring claims data and surveys of service members (Air Force Instruction 90-506, 2023; Keller et al., 2015; Marquis et al., 2017; Matthews, Hall, and Lim, 2015).

Self-Directed Harm and Suicide

DoD has also addressed harmful behaviors that are self-directed, including suicidal behavior. According to the 2020 DoD Suicide Event Report, the official reporting system for suicide events in the military services, there were 1,433 suicide attempts by 1,307 unique individuals in 2020, of which 384 resulted in death by suicide (DoD, OUSD[P&R], 2021, p. 4). For the active-component services, the 2020 DoD Suicide Event Report notes that firearm use was the most common method of injury, accounting for 65.9 percent of reported suicides, and that drug or alcohol overuse was the most common method of attempted suicide, accounting for 52.7 percent of suicide attempts in 2020 (DoD, OUSD[P&R], 2021, p. 1).

Although comparing the rates of suicide among service members with the rates among civilian employees or contractors is difficult because of different data sources and methods, data have shown that suicide among federal employees increased to a record high in 2018. According to the U.S. Bureau of Labor Statistics, suicides accounted for 28 percent of the 124 federal employee job-related deaths in 2018, and most of these employees were working in roles related to national security, particularly at the U.S. Department of Homeland Security ("BLS Data Provides Further Evidence of Suicide Epidemic in Federal Agencies," 2020).

In early 2023, one year after being established by the Secretary of Defense to conduct an evaluation of DoD efforts related to suicide, the Suicide Prevention and Response Independent Review Committee released a report with key recommendations (see Suicide Prevention and Response Independent Review Committee, 2023). Subsequently, in October 2023, the Secretary of Defense announced that DoD had modified and adopted the committee's recommendations (Austin, 2021). These recommendations ranged from modernizing prevention training and enhancing firearm safety to increasing access to mental health care and improving morale (DoD, 2023).

Another DoD-level policy document relevant to harmful behavior to self is DoDI 6490.16 (2017), *Defense Suicide Prevention Program*, which establishes the policies, responsibilities, and oversight of this Suicide Prevention Program. This DoDI also highlights policies for reporting suicides and suicide attempts and establishes both the Suicide Prevention General Officer Steering Committee and the Suicide Prevention and Risk Reduction Committee (DoDI 6940.16, 2017).

Additionally, DoDI 6400.09 (2020, p. 1) establishes policies aiming to "mitigate self-directed harm and prohibit abusive or harmful acts using a career-cycle perspective to promote enduring force readiness." Some of the primary prevention programs outlined in this DoDI include ones that address the needs of high-risk groups, that implement safety measures for high-risk on-base locations, that encourage personnel to seek help without stigma, and that provide advocacy, behavioral health, and other methods of recovery care (DoDI 6400.09, 2020, pp. 17–18).

DoDI 6400.09 (2020, p. 12) directs prevention personnel at the command or installation level to implement the self-directed harm prevention system; identify, adapt, implement, and evaluate research-based prevention programs; and consult and collaborate with leaders to optimize access and usage of resources related to prevention efforts. This DoDI also directs military leaders at the command and installation levels to do the same but also to encourage a culture of help-seeking and take actions that foster a command climate of dignity, respect, inclusion, and connectedness.

Best Practices for Preventing and Responding to Self-Directed Harm and Suicide

Evidence indicates that prevention activities to address suicide should focus on providing training that incorporates engaging, multimodal material and assesses performance in addition to ensuring access to treatment and other services and reducing toxic stress (Marquis et al., 2017; Maglione et al., 2021; Nash and Watson, 2012; Robson and Salcedo, 2014; Warlick et al., 2021; Zamorski, 2011). Military workplace activities associated with reducing toxic stress include limiting the duration or spacing of deployments, EAPs, financial counseling, and other military family support programs (Zamorski, 2011). Moreover, limiting access to the means to engage in the harmful behavior (e.g., alcohol, drugs, firearms) is associated with a decreased risk of suicide (Marquis et al., 2017). In 2023, the Suicide Prevention and Response Independent Review Committee presented ten broad recommendations to the Secretary of Defense aiming to "improve service member well-being by improving operations and infrastructure," as well as 117 specific recommendations in "four strategic directions of the Defense Strategy for Suicide Prevention: Healthy and Empowered Individuals, Families, and Communities; Clinical and Community Preventive Services; Treatment and Support Services; and Surveillance, Research, and Evaluation" (Suicide Prevention and Response Independent Review Committee, 2023, p. 6). In response to this committee's findings, the Secretary of Defense issued a memorandum outlining five lines of effort to prevent suicide in the military:

- foster a supportive environment
- improve the delivery of mental health care
- address stigma and other barriers to care
- revise suicide prevention training
- promote a culture of lethal means safety (Austin, 2023).

The literature shows that leadership should also address the key barriers to help-seeking and enhance the facilitators of care. Barriers to seeking help include logistical issues, mental health stigmas, and concerns about confidentiality and leader and coworker perceptions (Hamilton, Coleman, and Davis, 2017; LeFeber and Solorzano, 2019). Facilitators of care include leadership, family, and friends (Hom et al., 2017). A high level of trust among leadership and service members is associated with a significantly decreased suicide risk (Griffith, 2019).

After learning of potentially traumatic event or identifying suicidality, interventions should be initiated quickly, ideally within four days (Nash and Watson, 2012). This period is critical to frequently following up and providing access to treatment and social, physical, and other resources (Zamorski, 2011). *Psychological debriefing*, defined as "a structured, single-session, group intervention for early intervention after trauma" is discouraged and should be replaced by psychological first aid (Nash and Watson, 2012). Other evidence-based programs include collaborative care models, EAPs, and cognitive behavioral therapy if acute stress disorder has been diagnosed (Farmer, Whipkey, and Chamberlin, 2019). Other programs, such as resilience training and mindfulness, can decrease levels of distress and absenteeism but not the symptoms of mental health disorders (Maglione et al., 2021). Follow-ups should continue for approximately six months after an acute stress event, in addition to regular screenings in health programs (Nash and Watson, 2012).

Training, Education, and Programs

State of DoD Training: Joint Service Online Training

Service components, and varying echelons of command across the services, may require their workforces to take online courses available through Joint Knowledge Online as part of an onboarding process or for continuing education and training. If a service member is assigned to the Joint Staff, for instance, there are multiple courses assigned to them on entry to their position. These trainings may relate to broad categories, such as cyber security or anti-terrorism, or to more job- or command-specific trainings. This training process is similar for onboarding requirements at other DoD installations, offices, and units. Each functional and geographic CCMD has a list of trainings outlined in Joint Knowledge Online that its workforce is required to take on a periodic basis.[2]

RAND research on military sexual assault prevention and response training found that such training did not employ documented best practices: It was not comprehensive or of sufficient length; did not use varied, interactive teaching methods administered by well-trained

---

[2] USSPACECOM administers a course called Command Orientation and Mission Essential Training that all personnel in the command attend within 90 days of their arrival. The course is essentially "SPACECOM 101" and includes a senior leader mission brief, directorate-level mission briefs, and a joint assignment briefing. USSPACECOM's chaplain and Organizational Culture Team (which includes SAPR, MEO, and resiliency) also provide a briefing during this Command Orientation and Mission Essential Training.

prevention specialists; did not foster positive relationships; did not build both skills and knowledge; and did not include outcome evaluation, among other weaknesses (Acosta, Chinman, and Shearer, 2012, pp. 6–7).

With these caveats and the understanding that these trainings may not be the most effective way to train service members, it is still useful to document them for awareness of the training available online as of the writing of this report while integrated primary prevention is rolled out to address these concerns. Some of these Joint Knowledge Online trainings related to preventing and responding to harmful behaviors are listed in Appendix C.

Summary of Promising, Evidence-Based Resilience Programs

Prevention and response efforts for different harmful behaviors often overlap, and evidence supports the linkage among various challenges. Hazing, harassment, and sexual harassment are predictors of sexual assault (Marquis et al., 2017). Prevention actions that are aimed at harassment are associated with reduced toxic stress and mental health challenges (Zamorski, 2011). With all harmful behaviors, an organizational culture that discourages the behavior is critical to its prevention (Marquis et al., 2017).

Because these behaviors are linked, literature has supported a combined prevention strategy that addresses harmful behaviors holistically, with systematic standards and reporting protocols. This is why integrated primary prevention has begun rolling out across the services aiming to accomplish this holistic goal. DoDI 6400.09 (2020), *DoD Policy on Integrated Primary Prevention of Self-Directed Harm and Prohibited Abuse or Harm*, and DoDI 6400.11 (2020), *DoD Integrated Primary Prevention Policy for Prevention Workforce and Leaders*, outline the integrated primary prevention policies supporting these efforts. Adequate levels of staffing with investment should oversee these activities, and staffing could either be combined to oversee all harmful behaviors, or programs could be better integrated. Although some evidence-based programs have been developed to address harmful behaviors at large, as of this report's writing, most evidence-based programs or trainings target a specific harmful behavior. However, these specific programs include a multitude of relevant strategies to addressing harmful behaviors at large and improving workforce resilience. Appendix D describes some examples of these programs.

Ensuring the close collaboration among—and even co-location of—response professionals is another emerging best practice. The IRC recommended the co-location of SAPR and Sexual Harassment and Assault Response and Prevention (SHARP) programs with other special victim services, including the Family Advocacy Program, because co-located models are associated with high rates of provider and survivor satisfaction (DoD, 2021, p. 14). The "one-stop shop" model seeks to relieve burdens on those who come forward seeking support, to create personnel efficiencies, and to enhance privacy by placing sexual harassment and assault response services in buildings that also house services for less-stigmatized issues (DoD, 2021, pp. 14–17). This model may also enhance the recommended "no wrong door" approach and facilitate warm handoffs when victims are not certain about where they should turn, which can be a particular challenge in cases of harassment and joint-service environments (DoD, 2021, pp. 33–34).

CHAPTER 3

Workshop Approach and Results

In this chapter, we describe the workshop approach that we developed to understand the concerns surrounding resiliency, in which we conducted six workshops with a select number of participants from USSPACECOM personnel. This chapter has two parts. First, we present our approach, which includes the workshop facilitation guide that we developed, the sample of people who participated in these workshops, and how we coded the various themes that emerged from our notes of statements made by workshop participants.

Next, we describe the results from our coding of themes discussed during these workshops. We start with an overview of the key themes discussed during these workshops and then review examples of these key themes from each section of our workshops (i.e., resiliency challenges, who addresses these challenges, barriers for addressing these challenges, and proposed solutions to challenges).

From our limited sample of workshop participants, we found evidence that many of the resiliency challenges within USSPACECOM are similar to those found in other military contexts. One particular challenge for this CCMD, however, is that it is the newest among the CCMDs and its number of personnel is quickly growing. These organizational growing pains were a frequent topic of discussion, with concerns raised about logistical, career, and social or cultural barriers surrounding the branches of service and the CCMD. Most groups tended to focus on the role of leadership, improvements in communication, and creative approaches for improving training as some possible solutions for resiliency-related issues.

Methodological Approach

We designed the workshop facilitation plan, pretested it with current and former service members who have served in joint environments, and modified it in response to feedback. Then, we executed six workshops with stakeholders from USSPACECOM's headquarters during fall 2023. We conducted five of these workshops in person, while one session, which included both civilian employees and service members, was held online because of scheduling conflicts.

Appendix E displays the facilitation guide used for our workshops. This guide contains six key questions:

1. What challenges are you observing within USSPACECOM in regard to self-harm or suicide, sexual assault and sexual harassment, and hostile work environment?[1]
2. Can you provide examples of discrimination, self-harm or suicide, sexual assault and sexual harassment, or hostile work environment in USSPACECOM?[2]
3. In what aspects of prevention and response to these workforce challenges does USSPACECOM bear responsibility versus the military services?
4. What barriers exist to taking actions against discrimination, self-harm or suicide, sexual assault and sexual harassment, and hostile work environment?
5. What are the levers your leadership at USSPACECOM has the authority to pull that would improve the issues we discussed today?
6. Among those levers, what do you think USSPACECOM should do to better address these issues?

The design of our workshops shares similar features with focus groups. Both involve convening groups of participants who share similar features (e.g., civilian employees, service members), a facilitator who leads a discussion among participants, and a predetermined set of questions used to guide these discussions.

Workshops and focus groups differ in several ways, however (for an overview, see Larson, Grudens-Schuck, and Allen, 2004). First, the protocol used in workshops is designed in a way to promote a group discussion in which participants reach a consensus on solutions. In the case of our workshops, the protocol was designed to help participants reach a consensus on the potential solutions to the resiliency-related challenges that they raised. Second, the purpose of our small group discussions was primarily to generate ideas and solutions, not to promote divergent thinking or to disclose personal perceptions or behaviors.

Sample of Participants

Table 3.1 displays the convenience sample, or population of volunteers who took part in our six workshops. There was a total of 51 participants in all six workshops: 24 of them were civilian employees at USSPACECOM (47 percent), and the other 27 were service members assigned to this CCMD (53 percent). USSPACECOM selected a cross section of employees who were available and willing to participate, and we relied on USSPACECOM to recruit all participants.

---

[1] Discrimination is mentioned in the guide's "Background" section and discussed in the context of hostile work environment.

[2] Participants were asked to keep these examples focused on roles with the additional direction: "Please do not use individual identifiers, and instead, focus more on roles of those involved in response or the processes involved in addressing the situation."

TABLE 3.1

Total Number of Participants for Each Workshop

Group Number	Civilian Employees	Service Members
Group 1	10	—
Group 2	5	—
Group 3	9	—
Group 4	—	8
Group 5	—	10
Group 6	5	4
Total	29	22

NOTE: Group 6's workshop occurred online instead of in person like the others.

Table 3.1 shows how we organized the participants into six groups, three of which were all civilian employees, two of which were all military personnel, and one of which contained both military and civilian leaders. The mixed workshop group of civilian and military personnel convened online, while the other five groups interacted in person. Across all six groups, there was at least one participant associated with each of USSPACECOM's directorates.[3]

One member of our team served as a facilitator and followed the protocol reproduced in Appendix E. A second member of our team served as a notetaker for the comments made during the workshops without using personal identifiers. All in-person workshops occurred in the restricted areas of USSPACECOM, and our notetakers were required to use pen and paper instead of laptops or recording devices, which limited the details of their recorded comments. Therefore, the quotations included in this report are not necessarily verbatim and are intended to capture the gist of participants' statements. All information discussed during these workshops was unclassified.

Coding Scheme

We followed a four-step approach for coding the notes taken during the six workshops. First, two members of our team reviewed all the workshops' notes and manually coded key themes based on the six key questions listed in the facilitation guide.

Second, a member of our team used this initial review to develop a formal coding scheme and applied these codes to digital copies of the notes in Dedoose, a qualitative coding software. Third, a second member of the team who was not involved in this initial coding com-

---

[3] USSPACECOM has nine directorates: J0, Office of the Combatant Commander; J1, Human Capital; J2, Intelligence; J3, Global Space Operations; J4, Logistics and Engineering; J5, Strategy, Plans, and Policy; J6, Digital Superiority; J7, Joint Exercises and Training; and J8, Capability and Resource Integration.

pleted a coding test to validate intercoder reliability for the limited size of notes in our sample. Finally, this same team member reviewed the initial codes and met with the coder from the second step to adjudicate content that did not clearly fit within a particular code in the original coding scheme.

There are two limitations with the coding tests that we used in Dedoose to assess intercoder reliability. Primarily, we have a small sample size of workshops (i.e., we have notes for only six workshops). This small sample size makes estimates for intercoder reliability using Cohen's Kappa measure less reliable (Cohen, 1960). Additionally, not all codes were applicable across our small sample. For this reason, we selected two codes for the question about challenges that were applied across all our workshop groups—"diversity" and "culture"—and used these codes to conduct a coding test for our two independent coders. The results from this test showed that coders agreed 93.8 percent of the time for the application of the "diversity" code and 87.5 percent of the time for the application of the "culture" code.[4]

Descriptive Results

Table 3.2 displays the frequencies of the codes that we applied to our workshop notes. There are two types of codes displayed in this table. The first type is the *supra-code* that relates to a central theme in the key questions we asked workshop participants. There are four of these supra-codes: *challenges, responsibilities, barriers,* and *solutions.* The second type of code is a *specific code,* which represents a particular topic that was mentioned by multiple participants about each of these four themes. The frequencies displayed in Table 3.2 show the total number of times a code was applied to something that a participant said during our workshops.

Higher counts represent the prevalence of mentions, but some participants mentioned the same topic multiple times throughout the workshop. When these mentions occurred at different points in the conversation, we applied a separate code to each occurrence. Furthermore, in some cases, the topics mentioned by a few participants may have influenced what others decided to raise during these workshops. Thus, the frequencies in Table 3.2 represent an estimation of salient topics as described by a relatively small convenience sample of participants who decided to raise them within these groups.

The frequency of these supra-codes in Table 3.2 shows that *challenges* and *solutions* were the most common; there were 160 distinct mentions of resiliency challenges in USSPACE-COM and 100 distinct mentions of solutions to these challenges. This table also shows that these challenges—which was the supra-code with the greatest frequency—were largely related to "personnel issues" (36 mentions), "cohesion" within the CCMD (31 mentions), and "leadership" (24 mentions). For solutions, the participants' statements focused on "leadership"

---

[4] Despite being an unreliable estimate of intercoder reliability because of the small sample size (i.e., six workshop groups), the pooled Cohen's Kappa value for these coding tests was 0.76 for "diversity" and 0.67 for "culture."

TABLE 3.2
Summary of Codes Applied to Workshop Notes

Code	Frequency
Challenges	160
Personnel issues	36
Cohesion	31
Leadership	24
Culture	16
Inappropriate behaviors	15
Diversity	12
Training	9
No challenges	6
Miscellaneous	5
Mental health	5
Shaming	1
Responsibilities	32
Branches	12
CCMD	12
Individuals	4
Miscellaneous	3
Veterans' administration	1
Barriers	62
Logistical	21
Career	12
Social or cultural	12
Resources	11
Leadership	5
Miscellaneous	1
No barriers	0
Solutions	100
Leadership	34
Communications	28
Training	14
Team building	12
Staffing	10
Miscellaneous	2

NOTE: $N = 6$ workshops; codes were applied multiple times to the same workshop notes.

(34 mentions), "communications" within USSPACECOM (28 mentions), and "training" (14 mentions).

Overall, the workshop participants made fewer distinct comments about responsibilities (32 total mentions) and barriers (62 total mentions) than the other two supra-codes. For who is responsible for addressing challenges, there were an equal number of comments for both the service branches and USSPACECOM (12 mentions each). This suggests a mixed perception by participants about whether their service or the CCMD is the primary source of support for problems they observe at work. The most frequent comments about barriers to addressing problems were "logistical" (21 mentions), followed by "career" and "social or cultural" (12 mentions each).

In the following sections, we review examples of what participants said organized by the specific codes that we applied to their statements.

Summary of Comments Regarding Challenges

The top three specific codes that we applied to the theme of challenges are "personnel issues," "cohesion," and "leadership." These three challenges-related topics were the most frequently mentioned, while additional coded topics include "culture" with 16 distinct mentions, "inappropriate behaviors" with 15 mentions, and "diversity" with 12 mentions, among other topics.

Personnel Issues

The most salient topic related to challenges discussed during our workshops was personnel issues, which was mentioned 36 distinct times. Many of these issues related to growing pains accompanying the reestablishment of a CCMD, coupled with uncertainty over the decision about the location of USSPACECOM's headquarters.

As noted previously, USSPACECOM has been the newest CCMD since it was reconstructed in 2019. As a result, this CCMD has experienced various personnel challenges, which were discussed frequently during our workshops. For example, several participants mentioned challenges related to the identity of USSPACECOM and how some members of the public—and sometimes those in the U.S. military—confuse it with the U.S. Space Force. As one service member explained,

> At the sub-organization level, it gets confusing. Space Force does USSPACECOM missions. Now, I'm in Space Force for training. There's ambiguity in space given the newness of USSPACECOM. What's a task for which level?[5]

---

[5] All quotes in this chapter were derived from our workshop notes and represent what a participant said, but the statements are not necessarily verbatim.

Several participants also mentioned the role of the CCMD's growth and development when discussing challenges. As one service member noted, these challenges are typical of any new organization that is growing quickly, saying,

> Do people understand growing pains? It depends on the individual. Those with experience in organizations just starting [may understand]. Lower levels don't know what it takes; people can come here with unrealistic expectations. There is no slowing down.

One civilian employee noted that the challenges of these growing pains were mostly due to the lack of defined onboarding processes and instructions, claiming, "For new employees, there is lack of guidance or feedback. . . . I need feedback along the way."

Several civilian employees also noted concerns about the debate surrounding the canceled move of USSPACECOM headquarters from Colorado to Alabama. One remarked, "I was not moving regardless of the basing decision. I will retire by then." Another civilian expressed relief about the cancellation, commenting,

> I am new. There was a huge sigh of relief when they told us we are staying here and not moving to Alabama. Now we can fill empty billets. We joined as GS [General Schedule] civilians so we could not move every two years like the military. We are adults here, not 18-year-olds.

Cohesion

Another prominent discussion topic related to challenges was a lack of workforce cohesion, which was mentioned 31 distinct times. Several of the statements that we coded as "cohesion" related to the integration of service members, civil servants, and civilian contractors within USSPACECOM. As one civilian employee explained,

> This is my biggest issue: Contractors and civilians are so divided in this command. It was better at my old office. I hear that contractors say that "it's just the contractors who do all the work." That is demoralizing. I know we cannot gift or do awards in the same way, but people are not recognized for their work when they're contractors.

The issue of recognition for contractors was mentioned as a challenge by several participants. USSPACECOM relies heavily on contractors, but unlike civilian employees and service members, the contracts place constraints on the types of recognition that civilian contractors can receive. One civilian employee summarized this challenge by stating, "The contractor should be recognized. I have seen contractor work transferred to a civilian award and the civilian gets the credit instead." Similarly, another civilian employee noted,

> I don't know how the contracts are written. The J-[XX] cell, they come in their own time. They can't participate in outside activities like Resilience Day the way we can. Participat-

ing comes from their personal time. When they did a ribbon cutting, they wanted to give coins to a contractor. But they can't even do that. They cannot be recognized.

In addition to the issue of recognition, some participants raised concerns over the management of contractors in USSPACECOM. For example, one service member noted that contractors face limitations to their participation in team-related activities, such as training, and recommended,

> We need to make several efforts to make change, and contractors are a part of that, but they can't be part of training. We are having those conflicts, of not being able to include everyone in the team.

Leadership

The third-most-mentioned challenge during our workshops was the role of leadership. Overall, participants remarked on the confusion surrounding who is leading which process in USSPACECOM. For instance, one service member claimed that because of this confusion, some personnel default to their branch of service, saying that other CCMDs "may have figured it out, but we default to services and duplicate the work."

We specifically coded many of the challenges related to leadership as focused on policies, processes, and communication. For example, one civilian noted the need for greater input or explanation from leadership on resiliency programming by questioning, "How does this harm resilience? We had Resilience Week. We did volleyball and corn hole. I was not asked what I wanted to do for fun or resiliency."

A civilian employee similarly expressed frustration with the challenges regarding resiliency training by saying, "On Resilience Day, we would all be in the room to act on and learn what we shared. To me, [calling it] resilience was off. It was more of a team-building thing than resilience."

Additionally, several civilian employees raised concerns over the management of USSPACECOM's workforce of service members, civilian employees, and civil contractors. For instance, one civilian summarized the challenge of supervising different types of employees by saying,

> I see a lot of military members struggle with supervising civilians! It's a different way of managing. You can't just order them, you have to get buy-in. It's a big struggle. Many military supervisors managing civilians try to push that off to another civilian. It's strained. I rarely see civilians managing military members. We fudge structures sometimes so the military doesn't have to manage civilians.

Overall, the major theme regarding challenges from our workshop discussions was the relationships among different types of employees: service members, civil servants, and civilian contractors. When they were asked about challenges related to various harmful behaviors that may negatively influence resiliency at USSPACECOM, the participants tended to focus on topics primarily related to personnel issues, cohesion, and leadership.

In the next section, we review examples from our workshops that we coded as related to who is responsible for addressing these challenges within USSPACECOM.

Summary of Comments Regarding Responsibilities

When they were asked who bears the responsibility for harmful behavior prevention and response, our workshop participants equally pointed to the services and to USSPACECOM with 12 distinct mentions for each entity. Several participants claimed that both USSPACE-COM and the services bear some responsibility.[6] The participants' discussions about the services tended to focus on reporting channels and available resources, while their comments regarding USSPACECOM focused on culture creation, staffing, and who holds the "ultimate responsibility."

On the one hand, multiple workshop participants, especially those who are service members, described the services' role in building workforce resiliency. These participants described the services as being responsible for educating and training service members around harmful behaviors. Some service members described feeling more comfortable going to their own service to access resources or report misconduct than going to USSPACECOM. One participant shared,

> Each branch will default to their previous experience. There is a representative from each branch and people are more comfortable going to their own service. Fundamentally, the services are the same but use different terminology.

Some civilian participants also discussed responsibilities of the services and other entities outside USSPACECOM. For example, the role of the Air Force was noted. However, there was still some confusion among participants regarding where to receive support, even though the Secretary of the Air Force is listed as the CCSA for USSPACECOM. According to one civilian, "There was once a memo that the Air Force is the supporting agency for the command. It is not clear where we go."

The participants also discussed the differences among types of employers and employees. For instance, a participant employed by another DoD component mentioned some variations in training requirements, adding that "at [my component], we have our own avenue. We use our own reporting channels." Another participant also reported that there is a distinction between service members and civilians, specifically that "on the military end, it will go to

---

[6] The Secretary of the Air Force has been designated as the CCSA for USSPACECOM, with most relevant services for personnel located at Schriever and Peterson Space Force Bases. Not all USSPACECOM personnel are located on these installations. Some are in civilian office parks outside the bounds of installations. Furthermore, soldiers assigned to USSPACECOM may seek out various services at Fort Carson near Colorado Springs, Colorado.

that service lead. Civilians will fall to their direct line supervisor." However, one civilian claimed, "It's the services' responsibility to take care of people, though."

On the other hand, multiple service members described the essential role and responsibility of USSPACECOM in building workforce resilience and a culture of intolerance to harmful behaviors. As two participants noted, these efforts "should be command driven" and that "USSPACECOM holds responsibility. There are nuances among services, but the commander is ultimately responsible." Similarly, another participant stated,

> USSPACECOM has 100 percent responsibility for it. It is a command. It has responsibility for everything that happens here. Services should continue with what they're already doing, people are trained, they know what's expected, probably less so on the civilian side, but the commanding general is ultimately responsible.

Although some service members expressed a preference for receiving support through their own branch of service, as show in a previous quote, some expressed the opposite sentiment. One service member claimed, "I think members look to their direct supervisor or commanding officer. I don't think they look to the services." Several civilian participants also only looked to USSPACECOM leadership to address concerns. For example, one participant shared,

> I am an Air Force employee, but USSPACECOM is my workplace. I know nothing about the Air Force, only the combatant command. They handed me off. It has to be on leadership here, the combatant command, not the services.

Similarly, another civilian participant expressed that, because of the diverse workforce of service members, civilians, contractors, and military retirees and veterans, the "command has the responsibility to be a conduit to resources." As another participant shared, "It would be chaos if it was dispersed. We are a joint command."

Overall, the participants considered the responsibility for workplace challenges to be shared among three primary entities: the services, federal agencies (e.g., the Defense Intelligence Agency), and USSPACECOM. Some discrepancies emerged from the discussions, specifically for service members' preferred avenue of reporting issues and accessing resources, but most discussions mentioned the role of both the services and USSPACECOM leadership. However, this shared responsibility could be ambiguous in practice, limit the leadership's ability to take action, and result in logistical, career, or sociocultural barriers.

In the next section, we review the participants' commentary regarding these three frequently mentioned barriers to addressing challenges.

Summary of Comments Regarding Barriers

The top three specific codes that we applied to the theme of barriers are "logistical" with 21 distinct mentions, "career" with 12 mentions, and "social or cultural" with 12 mentions.

These three barriers were the most frequently mentioned, while additional coded barriers include "resources" with 11 distinct mentions and "leadership" with five mentions.

Logistical

The logistical concerns identified during the workshops focused largely on some of the same growing pains mentioned during discussions about challenges within USSPACECOM. For example, one service member described these logistical issues as a "tax" on well-being, claiming, "Some of the barriers include it being a new command, new systems, and logistical/computer issues are a huge tax on well-being. Before you even walk in, you feel negative."

Similarly, another participant from the services raised concerns about the CCMD's logistical processes, referencing contractors specifically and the process for submitting complaints or concerns about the contract. This service member said,

> For us, the biggest barrier ... [is] the rules and law with regards to contracting individuals. They are welcome to raise the issues with government leadership, but they are supposed to file complaints through the contract.

Several civilian participants also commented on logistical issues, mostly on the processes and a mixed understanding of who does what at USSPACECOM. One civilian explained, "We have to learn the things and processes. I have been here for one year and seen nothing on harassment. Not everyone knows how to address the issues they have." Another civilian noted that there are logistical burdens placed on those who report harassment, which may prove cumbersome in this CCMD. This participant explained,

> There are barriers to reporting. The victim of harassment bears a lot, and that takes too much effort. I was just doing my job and I have to take my time, telling the story over and over and explaining just a 30-second interaction of bad behavior. That person [the harasser] should be the one having to do paperwork and take the time. But that is the nature of the beast.

Career and the Risk of Retaliation

Another significant barrier discussed during the workshops was the implication and risk of retaliation on someone's career. Many of the participants' statements focused on the overall reporting system across DoD for inappropriate behaviors versus USSPACECOM-specific concerns. For example, several service members raised concerns about the implications for reporting inappropriate behaviors for themselves and for the person accused, which may disincentivize some people from raising concerns at all. One person expressed this frustration by saying, "How do people come forward? They could be putting their career on the line, so we need to break down barriers."

Similarly, several civilian participants also raised concerns and fears surrounding the potential ramifications if they were to report inappropriate behaviors. For instance, one civilian noted, "The atmosphere of regulations is a barrier. Someone's head is on the chopping block." Another civilian similarly claimed, "Fear of retribution from someone who is friends with anyone in the process is a barrier."

Social and Cultural Barriers

In addition to logistical and career-related barriers, social and cultural barriers were frequently mentioned during our workshops. Many statements related to the culture of USSPACECOM. For example, one civilian participant noted how a "storm cloud" informally follows reporting of self-directed harm by explaining,

> There are barriers to report or talk about self-harm. To say, "I have anxiety and depression," is not what I will always want. A storm cloud will follow me and there are whispers. If we don't allow people to talk freely, it is not good.

Another civilian noted that the relatively "flat" organizational structure of some teams in USSPACECOM can make it easier for peers to recognize harmful behaviors versus structures in larger CCMDs by outlining,

> This command will be large—it could be easy to become anonymous—we're a flat organization in my team, with GS [General Schedule] 13s, 14s, and 15s, it's incumbent on the front-line supervisor to notice [struggling employees]. I feel really part of the team here, compared to where I was before. Someone would notice and be concerned if I seemed down, more than in my last command, where no one would've noticed; I could've stepped in front of a train, and they only would've noticed that I didn't show up to work.

The service members also raised concerns about social dynamics serving as a cultural barrier but pointed out how this is not unique to USSPACECOM and exists across the military. For instance, one participant said, "Some barriers include social dynamics and if others haven't taken action. You don't want to be a problem person and don't want to rock the boat. There can be cultural differences in what is acceptable in one service versus others." Similarly, another member noted the stigma surrounding speaking up about concerning behaviors by claiming, "Maybe we should speak up, but it can be hard to 'be that person' and make people feel uncomfortable. Stigma can make it hard to speak up if it's 'not a big deal.'"

Overall, the most frequently mentioned barriers during our workshops were issues that were logistical, which relate to other concerns surrounding the history and size of USSPACE-COM; career-related, which are commonly observed across the military; and social or cultural, which are also common in military contexts. In other words, many of the barriers discussed during our workshops are not unique to USSPACECOM but similar to barriers found in other parts of the U.S. military.

Summary of Comments Regarding Solutions

The top three specific codes that we applied to the theme of solutions are "leadership" with 34 distinct mentions, "communications" with 28 mentions, and "training" with 14 mentions.

"Team building" and "staffing" were also mentioned 12 times and 10 times, respectively. The leadership-related solutions focused on clarity, the communications-related solutions related to the accessibility and sharing of resources, and the training-related solutions mostly concerned how to train more effectively.

Leadership

Among the participants, the service members reported that their leadership's current action for supporting resiliency is an articulation of the policy. One participant confirmed that this articulation takes place routinely by saying, "Normally, leadership will just speak to a group or division. A zero tolerance policy is articulated."

The civilian participants discussed their need for a more unified plan that increases workforce resilience in USSPACECOM. There was a sense among these workshop participants that their leadership did not know how to cultivate or build better resiliency. One participant claimed, "A crawl-walk-run plan from leadership would be great. But they don't know how to get there."

The civilian participants also emphasized the need for transparency in their leaders' plans for resilience, with one person describing how "transparency for a command is huge." Generally, the civilians felt that soliciting help from USSPACECOM members would help make their plans transparent in addition to helping leadership improve their resilience implementation plans. One participant summarized this sentiment by saying, "They just need to be honest and tell us and help get our input."

Communications

In addition to leadership, our workshop participants next most frequently spoke about communications as a solution for improved resiliency. The ability to communicate which services are available and where was described as especially challenging for USSPACECOM, because its offices are geographically dispersed. Without a central, accessible hub for all resiliency services, some workforce members may not know about or may not be able to access these services. In general, participants stated they wanted more awareness and simple communications about the available resilience-related services, such as "an email explaining the process" or "bulletin boards with Chaplain, OneSource, etc."

Several participants also identified the need to communicate the existence and location of services at each base. For instance, one participant said,

> For garrison services, in-processing is at Schriever. They need to go to Right Start on Peterson. It was a good 8-hour day. They don't talk about Ft. Carson, but people here probably need to know about it, and they should probably broadcast Ft. Carson services too.

In addition to the basic communication of services, multiple civilian participants suggested hosting forums where discussions of viewpoints and more community announcements could take place. One civilian suggested, "We need to know who the points of contact are. We need an open conversation to talk about our viewpoints. If you don't hear others' views, you will never change. That could be held on a Teams meeting." Furthermore, another civilian recommended, "We need a speech or to talk regularly to give ourselves a chance to reflect on the past rather than training events."

Finally, the participants wanted a way to preserve privacy while still communicating to the workforce that the harassment and hostile work environment policies were being enforced and that any perpetrators were being held accountable. They felt that increased communications would both encourage reporting and discourage bad behavior. For example, one participant commented, "There have to be DoD policies on repercussions—privacy matters, but it [news/gossip about these things] gets around—we need to know, publicly acknowledge, that command is trying to do something about it or see an email that it's being handled." Similarly, another participant said,

> You can't do public floggings—you can't have a town hall with public shaming—but how can you get it out that it *is* happening and someone was punished? . . . This [specific situation where people had been caught and held accountable] would encourage victims to come forward and discourage perpetrators.

Training

Coupled with clarifying leadership and improving communication, our workshop participants spoke frequently about resiliency trainings. The participants offered many ideas for how to better execute trainings for a resilient workforce. There was agreement among both service members and civilians that in-person trainings were far more effective and superior to online or computerized trainings. For instance, one participant said, "I like the idea of having a town hall. In person is more impactful for training events."

The participants thought that online resilience trainings would get lost in the mix of the many other online trainings and would have very little practical effect. As an example, one person said, "I like group trainings. In the combatant command, we have more senior people, retirees. You blow it off when it's online, you have done it 50 times."

In-person, small-group trainings tailored to the specific employee mix, however, would have greater effect, according to several participants, and show to USSPACECOM employees that resiliency in the CCMD's workforce is valued. One person suggested, "More mandatory training isn't great. Innovative small-group training is needed for it to be taken seriously." Another participant agreed, adding, "And it gets buy-in, shows people you're engaged with employees and care more."

Our workshop participants also recommended that in-person trainings could be even more powerful if relevant, updated examples were used. These trainings could be given by representatives of the relevant offices promoting workforce resiliency, including SAPR and MEO or EEO offices. For example, one participant suggested,

> We all do online training. Instead, you could implement in-person trainings and focus on what's applicable to the command, specifically, because they're old and much of it isn't

applicable anymore. Bringing in relevant examples more current to the command would help. Use resources we have [pointed at the in-house SAPR and EO representatives who were in the room] more efficiently versus standard online training that I forget.

Additional ideas from participants for how to make resilience-related trainings more successful included getting the right size and mix of participants in each training session, as well as the proper timing of trainings. For such a training, one person recommended, "Hold it at the division level. Some will be bigger than others, but around 15–20 people." Several participants also mentioned the need to ensure that the trainings were not so small that conversation and sharing was difficult but also not so large that participants were lost in a crowd. One person summarized this difficulty with size by saying, "Too small, and there's no sharing. Too big, and it's just 'check the box.'"

Some participants encouraged in-person training that invites workers from across divisions to the same session. This was to encourage cross-pollination of experiences and ideas from across USSPACECOM. One participant used our workshop as an example by stating that "it's good to cross divisions to share perspectives across units, like this [gestures around the table]."

Furthermore, multiple participants suggested that the timing for these in-person sessions be twice a year, so that most or all employees had the chance to attend at least one session. One person cautioned against having too many trainings by saying, "Maybe twice a year? More often than that, and people will disengage." Another person agreed, stating "Two in-person trainings per year means everyone will get at least one, even with leave and TDY [temporary duty]."

While they generally agreed that in-person training was best, USSPACECOM participants from the military also emphasized preventative measures in building a more resilient workforce. Some military participants encouraged additional education more broadly on the different work styles of employees in ways that can help bridge generational gaps and other differences among workers. One service member summarized this approach as "across-the-board education efforts to cultivate a positive workplace environment for all, in case people don't speak up, or for those who don't know they are insulting, age gap issues."

A few military participants discussed the need to host trainings on how to handle difficult conversations. This type of preventative measure could support a more resilient workforce by proactively reducing the barriers and discomfort for superiors and victims in dealing with workforce members who create hostile work environments. One service member described this type of training by saying,

> What I've seen a lot here and other places is knowing how to have those hard conversations. Some people are good with them, some people avoid them. There are plenty of workshops to help you through a hard conversation. I think those are really needed.

Another participant concurred with this sentiment, adding,

> Is there enough training? I haven't seen anything in this command. I've seen stuff in other places. I've seen two workshops on hard conversations, one using role-play. It was based on a book about hard conversations. It's best with people in the workshop and better when it's not with coworkers.

Overall, the workshop participants agreed on several solutions to creating a more resilient workforce at USSPACECOM. These include leadership developing a clear plan and sharing it transparently with all employees; the communication of both basic information about access to resilience-related services, as well as reassurances that anti-harassment policies are being carried out; and in-person trainings, with the right size, mix, and timing, along with some preventative measures. All together, these solutions presented by the participants would help the USSPACECOM workforce become more resilient.

Summary of Key Takeaways from Workshops

To summarize, we organized a series of workshops with a convenience sample of both service members and civilians from USSPACECOM. To identify the various problematic behaviors that may undermine resiliency, we asked participants about the challenges they see to enhancing resiliency, who is responsible for addressing problems and taking actions, the barriers to addressing these challenges, and their ideas for solutions.

The following is a summary of our key takeaways from the participants' answers to our six workshop questions:

- **Challenges:** The top challenges are personnel issues largely related to growth in personnel within USSPACECOM; a lack of cohesion among service members, civilians, and civilian contractors; and knowing who is leading which process in the CCMD.
- **Responsibilities:** The participants were equally divided in identifying whether USSPACECOM or their branch of service is responsible for addressing problems and taking actions, although some pointed to both, while others referenced the role of federal agencies (e.g., the Defense Intelligence Agency).
- **Barriers:** The obstacles mentioned during the workshops included logistical barriers regarding who does what; a possible career risk of retaliation, which is a broader issue in DoD; and sociocultural barriers in reporting harmful behaviors (e.g., stigma, social dynamics), which is also a broader issue in DoD.
- **Solutions:** The participants' ideas focused on the role of leadership in supporting various resiliency efforts, especially being transparent to civilians and service members alike, as well as the role of communications regarding which resources were available, where these resources existed, and how the CCMD carries out various resiliency efforts. Furthermore, multiple participants mentioned the need for more engaging, in-person trainings on workforce resilience-related topics.

CHAPTER 4

Conclusion and Recommendations

USSPACECOM was reestablished in 2019 to defend national interests and security in space. Since its early days, the CCMD has faced significant external pressure because of the proposed relocation of its headquarters and the subsequent controversial decision to cancel this move. Meanwhile, USSPACECOM has grown quickly, although the workforce size is expected to remain relatively stable through 2025. Furthermore, the composition of its workforce is diverse, evenly split among civilian employees, contractors, and service members from across the military services, all with their own cultures, policies, and procedures. Therefore, enhancing resiliency and mitigating harmful behaviors are critical goals as this CCMD reaches full operational capability.

During our workshops with current USSPACECOM personnel, which included both military and civilian personnel, we found that many of the issues surrounding harmful behaviors are similar to those in other military contexts. Some cases of inappropriate behavior, hostility, and lack of diversity were discussed among workshop participants, but harmful behaviors across USSPACECOM, including discrimination, sexual assault, and sexual harassment, were not frequently discussed, as evidenced by our coding of the participants' statements. When asked about these behaviors, the participants tended to focus on organization-related issues for how USSPACECOM addresses harmful behaviors rather than on specific instances of them. Our discussions were with a limited convenience sample of USSPACECOM personnel, and furthermore, results from our workshops should not be taken as evidence for a low prevalence of harmful behaviors at USSPACECOM.

Nonetheless, barriers to reporting harmful behaviors and to seeking help after traumatic events still exist, in addition to other challenges. Overall, the most prominent theme related to resiliency barriers discussed in these workshops was organizational. Thus, if we return to the social-ecological framework for resilience (see Figure 1.4), the key challenges for USSPACECOM are located at the "organizational" level. The location of these challenges suggests the need for USSPACECOM to continue investing in a "one-stop shop" that links the various resilience-related programs that are designed to support service members, civil servants, and civilian contractors.

Logistical and social or cultural concerns were also frequently discussed as barriers to responses or help, which were described as also present in other military contexts. As explained in our review of DoD policies on harmful behavior, the responsibilities for addressing these problems are decentralized. Likewise, USSPACECOM personnel in our workshops acknowledged a shared responsibility among this CCMD, the services, and OSD.

Similar to personnel in most other CCMDs, USSPACECOM personnel may need to access resources that are not housed within the CCMD itself, such as those available from their military branches or from other employer-provided support systems. For example, personnel may access behavioral health care from military treatment facilities, community providers, the U.S. Department of Veterans Affairs, or an EAP, depending on their coverage and eligibility. Unlike most other CCMDs, however, USSPACECOM has an Organizational Culture Team consisting of an EO coordinator, an SAPR program manager, and a resilience program manager who can respond to hostile work environment, sexual assault, and other resilience-related concerns. Unique among the CCMDs, USSPACECOM's information about in-house professionals is easily available and accessible from a dropdown menu on its homepage, signaling this CCMD's commitment to providing these services.[1] Expanding the awareness of and consistent access to these USSPACECOM-level services, despite personnel being dispersed across multiple locations, will become increasingly important as this CCMD grows.

Recommendations

Our workshop participants agreed that both leadership and communications are the basis for solutions to the various challenges that exist in USSPACECOM. Several workshop participants spoke positively about the clear and robust messaging from leadership about these topics, as well as overall proactive leadership presence. Furthermore, the diverse nature of USSPACECOM's workforce, which includes service members, civil servants, and contractors, may require additional communications from leadership for clarity on the various types of resilience-related resources that are available to certain classes of employees without excluding anyone. Contractors, specifically, are a large part of USSPACECOM's workforce, have the potential to remain a sizable proportion of the workforce for the foreseeable future, and can contribute greatly to USSPACECOM's culture of resilience. However, contractors are not included in most resilience-building workplace activities. Therefore, our first recommendation addresses this concern.

Recommendation 1: USSPACECOM should streamline, target, and formalize communications about various resilience-building efforts to different classes of personnel within this CCMD.

This recommendation involves developing a clear plan for enhancing workforce resilience through a process that continually solicits feedback from all types of employees, demonstrates

---

[1]   Special Operations Command has a link to its Force and Family Readiness program from the homepage dropdown menu; the first three resources listed after navigating to that page are for a Child ID Kit, Family Disaster Planning Guide, and Headquarters Commandant Office Trifold. The Southern Command and Africa Command websites have links that lead to information about the Army's overall SHARP or SAPR program and the closest garrison program.

the leadership's commitment to these efforts, and shares the plan transparently and regularly with the workforce, which were all important themes from our literature review and workshops. This plan also involves formalizing communications about resilience efforts, perhaps through dedicated websites, links from CCMD's homepage to those resilience websites, newsletters, or periodic resilience-related stories in USSPACECOM-wide communications, its external website, or any internal websites, as well as prominent signage in buildings. These communication channels were described as particularly helpful in our workshops.

Recommendation 2: USSPACECOM's contracting officer should include language in professional service contracts to clarify what types of resiliency-related resources, team building, training, and professional recognition are available to civilian contractors.

According to our workshop findings, USSPACECOM should consider writing contractor eligibility into contracts to extend workforce resilience resources for when contractors are not eligible for some of these resources. Such changes require a separate evaluation of relevant federal contract language. One starting point to consider is reviewing the language in the U.S. Space Command Instruction 1101.01F (2022), *Personnel Recognition Program*, which could be amended to apply to government contractors for certain award recognitions. While overarching DoD policy places limits on contractor recognition for monetary and non-monetary awards, DoDI 1400.25 (Vol. 451, 2013, pp. 13, 24) lists conditions for which contractors may be recognized for awards.

As a reconstructed CCMD, there is evidence of growing pains within the organizational structure of USSPACECOM. Most generally, its diverse workforce does not always know who does what regarding various resilience-related topics or issues. To our knowledge, USSPACECOM is one of the only unified CCMDs with its own personnel dedicated to resiliency. Because USSPACECOM is geographically dispersed, building accessibility can be complicated, and desired signage in some buildings is prohibited. Having a central, accessible hub for all resilience-related services might increase the workforce's overall access to these services. Furthermore, this approach of a one-stop shop for resiliency could become a model for other CCMDs to implement. This recommendation is supported by our literature review, which showed the importance of access to services and reporting channels in addition to allocating sufficient funding and staffing to these efforts. Given the array of services in the services and OSD, we conclude that there is a need to simplify and streamline these services for the individual employee. To this end, we recommend the following.

Recommendation 3: USSPACECOM should continue to invest in developing a one-stop shop for strengthening resiliency at USSPACECOM that connects service members, civil servants, and civilian contractors to all available resources across the entire DoD enterprise.

As USSPACECOM grows, there will be the increased need to invest in scaling a one-stop shop for resiliency. Offering these services within the CCMD, where in-house professionals can maintain awareness of services available to the entire USSPACECOM workforce at nearby garrisons and within the local community, is a potential best practice that should be shared. As design decisions about a permanent headquarters are finalized, planners should ensure convenient accessibility to and continued co-location of resiliency team members.

In addition, as DoD and the services roll out integrated primary prevention, the existing EO, SAPR, and resilience personnel at USSPACECOM should work to prevent duplication of effort and to maximize collaboration on the shared goals of reducing risk and boosting protective factors.

Finally, targeted training is a useful tool for any USSPACECOM-specific resiliency strategy. Our literature review found that high-quality training should be varied, use interactive teaching methods administered by well-trained prevention specialists, and build both skills and knowledge (Acosta, Chinman, and Shearer, 2012, pp. 6–7). Several participants in our workshops mentioned their desire for an engaging training session that is in person and in a small group rather than online or lecture-based presentations. For example, the use of interactive tabletop exercises and group activities to help personnel understand why resiliency efforts are useful and when to use them could be effective across the CCMD. For these reasons, we offer Recommendation 4.

Recommendation 4: Personnel in USSPACECOM's one-stop shop for resilience-building programs should develop interactive, engaging, and targeted training on resiliency that meets the unique needs of its workforce.

This last recommendation asks USSPACECOM to consider allowing contractor time to be covered in its contracts to enable this portion of the workforce to also attend these trainings.

In conclusion, USSPACECOM has a unique opportunity to build a one-stop shop for resiliency among the CCMDs. By simplifying the connection among this CCMD and the variety of resiliency services that exist across the U.S. military, in addition to further experimentation with outreach methods, USSPACECOM's resiliency program could become a template for how other unified CCMDs strengthen resiliency among their own workforces.

APPENDIX A

Background on U.S. Combatant Commands

The U.S. military has 11 CCMDs, each of which executes a broad ongoing mission under a single commander. CCMDs' missions are designated by the President via the Secretary of Defense on the advice of the chairman of the Joint Chiefs of Staff. To date, these CCMD missions are defined either by function (e.g., special operations, transportation, or cyber) or by geography (e.g., Africa, Europe, Space).

Figure A.1 shows the 11 geographic and functional CCMDs, as of 2023.

FIGURE A.1

Geographic and Functional U.S. Combatant Commands, 2023

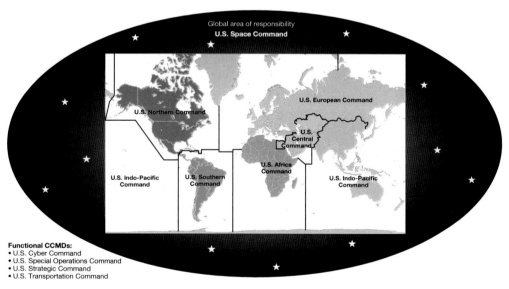

SOURCE: Adapted from U.S. Department of the Air Force, 2022.

As the figure shows, there are seven commands whose missions are defined by geographic location:

- U.S. Northern Command
- U.S. Southern Command
- U.S. European Command
- U.S. Central Command
- U.S. Africa Command
- U.S. Indo-Pacific Command
- U.S. Space Command.

There are an additional four commands whose missions are defined by function:

- U.S. Cyber Command
- U.S. Special Operations Command
- U.S. Strategic Command
- U.S. Transportation Command.

The parameters of responsibilities of these CCMDs can change over time as national security concerns evolve. For example, Alaskan Command was created in 1947 to defend Alaska following World War II (Joint Base Elmendorf-Richardson, undated). However, that command was disestablished in 1975, and its area of responsibility is now part of U.S. Northern Command. Similarly, USSPACECOM was created in 1985 in response to threats during the Cold War (Lopez, 2019). This CCMD was ultimately folded into U.S. Strategic Command in 2002, before being reestablished in 2019 by then-President Donald Trump.

Literature Review Methods

In January and February 2023, we searched DoD, academic, and technical literature focused on the four categories of harmful behaviors identified by USSPACECOM as key areas of concern: discrimination, sexual assault and harassment, hostile work environment, and self-directed harm. These four categories are described in Table B.1.

DoD Literature Search and Selection Strategy

We searched military literature to identify current policies, procedures, and trends in harmful behavior. We searched the DoD Executive Services Directorate for DoD directives and instructions, the DoD Office of People Analytics for reports and statistics, the Defense Technical Information Center for other military literature, several service component publications sites (i.e., the Army Publications Directorate) for service-specific directives and guidance, and CCMD resource pages for location- and command-specific policies and resources.

Academic and Technical Literature Search and Selection Strategy

To identify best practices and programs for preventing and responding to harmful behaviors, we searched peer-reviewed academic literature via PubMed, PsycINFO, and Embase.

TABLE B.1
Harmful Behaviors and Threats to Resilience for USSPACECOM

Broad Category	Harmful Behaviors and Threats to Resilience
Discrimination	Gender-based, sexual, racial, and other forms of intolerance and EEO violations
Sexual assault and harassment	Unwanted or offensive oral, written, or physical behavior of a sexual nature
Hostile work environment	Workplace violence, bullying, and hazing
Self-directed harm	Self-inflicted injuries and suicide

We also identified technical reports (i.e., RAND reports), and as a supplementary strategy, we searched Google Scholar and reviewed bibliographies of articles identified for inclusion.

We reviewed titles and abstracts to assess eligibility criteria. Eligible populations were composed of U.S. military service members and leaders, as well as members of other relevant organizations, such as foreign militaries, federal government and emergency response agencies, and sports teams. The included interventions involved training, education, and other workplace initiatives aimed at addressing workplace challenges. Epidemiological articles that focused on the nature or trends of the problems were not included. The outcome indicators included but were not limited to prevention best practices, changes in the harmful behavior in question, and barriers and facilitators to change. For the included articles, we abstracted key study characteristics. These characteristics included setting, challenge of interest, program name and description (if applicable), study description, method, primary findings, and key recommendations. We then grouped study findings and recommendations into three categories: preventing, reporting, and responding. Our results are presented in Table B.2.

In total, 52 academic articles and technical reports were identified for inclusion. Of these 52 articles, 27 of them had information on sexual assault and harassment, 16 on self-directed harm or suicide, 15 on discrimination, 14 on hostile work environment. These categories are not mutually exclusive; some articles discussed multiple challenges. For example, sexual assault and harassment were discussed along with discrimination ($n = 3$) and hazing or bullying ($n = 2$). One article focused on all four categories. The context of a majority ($n = 27$) of articles was the military at large, followed by the Air Force ($n = 9$), Army ($n = 6$), Marine Corps ($n = 3$), and law enforcement agencies ($n = 2$).

TABLE B.2

Academic and Technical Literature Search Strategy

Topic	Limiters Applied	Search Terms
Discrimination	Search domain: title/abstract	(discrimination or racism or sexism or ableism) AND (military or soldiers or armed forces or service members or navy or army or air force)
Sexual assault and harassment	Search domain: title/abstract	(sexual assault or sexual harassment) AND (military or soldiers or armed forces or service members or navy or army or air force)
Hostile work environment	Search domain: title/abstract	(hostile workplace or interpersonal violence or workplace violence or bullying or hazing) AND (military or soldiers or armed forces or service members or navy or army or air force)
Self-directed harm	Search domain: title/abstract	(suicide or self-harm or self-directed harm or psychological resilience or toxic stress) AND (military or soldiers or armed forces or service members or navy or army or air force) AND (intervention or prevention or reduction or response)

APPENDIX C

Joint Knowledge Online Courses on Harmful Behaviors

Table C.1 lists some of the courses available through Joint Knowledge Online, organized by the type of topic, including the prefix for the course on Joint Knowledge Online, the course's number, and the course's name and length. This list is not comprehensive.

TABLE C.1

Joint Knowledge Online Courses on Harmful Behaviors

Type	Prefix	Course Number	Course Name (Length)
Sexual assault and harassment	DEOMI-	ATS-3000	Sexual Assault Prevention and Response (1 hour)
	DHA-	US695	Interpersonal Violence Response for Healthcare Personnel (1.5 hours)
	JS-	US021	Joint Staff Sexual Assault Prevention and Response Training (1 hour)
	PREV-	002	Sexual Assault in the Military and the Way Forward (1.5 hours)
	SAPRO-	CATCH01	To CATCH a Serial Offender (CATCH) Program Introduction Training (0.75 hour)
	USN-	RTC3.03	Sexual Assault Prevention and Response (1 hour)
	PREV-	WEB11	Understanding Sexual Harassment and Shifting the Paradigm Towards Civility (1.5 hours)
	DCPAS-	001	Preventing Workplace Violence for Employees (1.5 hours)
	DCPAS-	002	Preventing Workplace Violence for Supervisors (2 hours)
	DHA-	US481	Anti-Harassment Workplace Training (0.5 hour)
	MCSD-	SHARP-001	Sexual Harassment Assault Response and Prevention (SHARP) (3 hours)

Table C.1—Continued

Type	Prefix	Course Number	Course Name (Length)
EEO	JS-	US013	Joint Staff Military Equal Opportunity Policy Basic Training (1 hour)
	JMESI-	US067	Leadership Fourteen: Creating a Culturally Sensitive Workplace (1 hour)
	DEOMI-	ATS-2040	Age Discrimination (1 hour)
Resilience	JMESI-	US070	Leadership: Resilience, Wellness, and Cooperation (1 hour)
Suicide	JS-	US006	Joint Staff Suicide Awareness and Prevention (1 hour)
	DHA-	US1146	Navy Suicide Prevention Training for Providers (UNCLASSIFIED//FOUO) (2 hours)

SOURCE: Features information from Joint Knowledge Online, undated.

Programs to Address Harmful Behaviors

From our review of the literature, we identified several evidence-based programs that could be potentially relevant to USSPACECOM, including programs that could be implemented in full or in part or that are currently implemented within a service branch. This appendix describes programs intended to address harmful behaviors within the U.S. military and beyond. We did not identify programs specific to discrimination or hostile work environment, only hazing, but we did identify broader programs that could be applied to these behaviors.

Programs for All Harmful Behaviors

Bystander Intervention: This program places the responsibility of intervening on *all* service members, not only the victims and perpetrators (Centers for Disease Control and Prevention, 2016; Gedney et al., 2018; Holland and Cipriano, 2019; Potter and Stapleton, 2012; Stander and Thomsen, 2016). It should be noted that rank, gender, training experience, and leadership responses affect an individual's willingness to report as a third-party witness. Therefore, different reporting strategies or channels may be needed for different ranks.

Getting to Outcomes©: The ten steps of Getting to Outcomes can assist with the planning, implementation, evaluation, and sustainment of prevention and response to harmful behaviors (Chinman et al., 2020).

Mindfulness Approaches: *Mindfulness* has been defined as "a mental mode characterized by full attention to present-moment experience without elaboration, judgment, or emotional reactivity" (Johnson et al., 2014, p. 845). This approach entails providing examples and instruction to promote this mental mode. Evidence shows that mindfulness may improve emotion regulation, impulse control, and workplace morale (Hepner et al., 2022; Johnson et al., 2014; Maglione et al., 2021).

Sexual Assault and Harassment Prevention Programs

STOP SV: A Technical Package to Prevent Sexual Violence: This Centers for Disease Control and Prevention report identifies prevention practices with best evidence (Centers for Disease Control and Prevention, 2016). Relevant practices include promoting peer norms (e.g., bystander approaches), training around skills (e.g., empowerment training), creating an accountable culture (e.g., consistent application of policies, reporting, and monitoring), and supporting victims (e.g., client-centered treatments).

Healthy Relationship Approaches to Sexual Assault Prevention: This study provides an overview and guide to developing skills (Farris et al., 2021). Dating violence prevention, sexual risk reduction programs, women's empowerment programs, and others include interactive features, such as scenarios, role-play, small-group sessions, and writing exercises.

Hazing Training for Leaders

A Commander's Guide to Hazing Prevention: This short guide for military commanders provides definitions of hazing, common situations involving hazing, barriers to reporting, and key prevention and response strategies (Matthews, Hall, and Lim, 2015).

Hazing Prevention and Response: Training for Military Leaders: Similar to the guide for commanders, this interactive presentation is a training tool for leaders to learn more about hazing and evidence-based prevention and response activities (Keller et al., 2017).

Psychological Support and Suicide Prevention Programs

Psychological First Aid: The aim of this technique is to "stop the bleeding" in psychological distress among those experiencing high-stress reactions to acute situations rather than all service members or even high-risk individuals. The key elements of psychological first aid include "(1) contact and engagement, (2) safety and comfort, (3) stabilization (if needed), (4) information gathering, (5) practical assistance, (6) connection with social supports, (7) information on coping, and (8) linkage to collaborative services" (Nash and Watson, 2012, p. 642). Evidence shows that this program increases resilience and psychological health among service members, particularly after an acute stress event or experience with suicidality (Farmer, Whipkey, and Chamberlin, 2019; Nash and Watson, 2012).

EAPs: The primary purpose of an EAP is "strategic guidance, support, and consultation offered internally to an organization or through an external provider to assist with personal or family issue" (Farmer, Whipkey, and Chamberlin, 2019, p. xi). EAP services range from short-term counseling and financial advice to health and wellness information. Evidence shows that these programs increase resilience and psychological health in the workplace (Zamorski, 2011).

Holistic Health and Fitness: This program, which was piloted in the Army, integrates five health and performance areas: physical, mental, sleep, nutrition, and spiritual. Various experts are involved in Holistic Health and Fitness, including strength and conditioning coaches, behavioral health professionals, dieticians, and chaplains. Early evidence shows that this program reduced the number of suicides by 37 percent among soldiers in units that implemented the program (South, 2023).

UNITE: UNITE was developed by the Air Force Services Center with the goal of enhancing unit cohesion (Holliday et al., 2022). Airmen and commanders indicated a high level of satisfaction with the program, and commanders reported that community cohesion coordinators were valuable resources. Better publicizing of UNITE was considered a key area of improvement.

Workshop Facilitation Guide

The following is a reproduction of the facilitation guide used for our workshops. It has not been edited for grammar, syntax, spelling, or formatting.

FACILITATION PLAN
DRAFT DATE: August 18, 2023

1.	Pre-Workshop time for participants to arrive	-00:15
2.	**Welcome and Overview; Introductions** **BACKGROUND** • We are research staff from the RAND Corporation, a non-partisan and non-profit research organization that develops solutions to public policy problems. RAND is home to the National Defense Research Institute, a Federally-Funded Research and Development Center for the Office of the Secretary of Defense. • USSPACECOM asked RAND to convene a diverse set of stakeholders within the Command to discuss workforce resiliency. We are focusing on elements that can harm resiliency, including discrimination, self-harm or suicide, sexual assault and sexual harassment, and hostile work environment. We are holding workshops to discuss problems, solutions, and barriers to solutions at USSPACECOM regarding preventing or responding to these workforce resiliency challenges.	0:00 – 00:10

- We recognize that the services are hiring a prevention workforce and rolling out various prevention and response initiatives in response to recommendations made by two recent Independent Review Commissions. In addition, we realize that USSPACE-COM is still working toward full operational capability. As the newest unified combatant command, USSPACECOM has a unique opportunity to design and implement systems and policies to maximize workforce resiliency.
- The goal of these workshops is to bring together stakeholders, discuss topics related to self-harm or suicide, sexual assault and sexual harassment, and hostile work environment in USSPACE-COM, and identify actionable solutions and any barriers to those solutions.

There will be six overarching questions, which will focus on challenges in these threats to resilience, who bears responsibility for prevention and response, barriers to taking action, and levers that USSPACECOM leadership could pull to better address these issues.

LOGISTICS

- The Chatham House Rule applies, so we will not audio or video record these conversations. While we will take notes, we will not list your name or affiliation in these notes. We ask that everyone here not to discuss what others said in the future. The final product from these workshops will be a short report that we will share with USSPACECOM and the public.

INTRODUCTIONS

- Before we dive into the discussion, let's go around the room and introduce ourselves with our names and roles.

3.	**Question 1: What challenges are you observing within USSPACE-COM in regard to self-harm or suicide, sexual assault and sexual harassment, and hostile work environment?** • *Facilitator Note: Each Facilitator should have 2-3 examples of the focused issues.* – *Listen. Solicit responses from participants who haven't spoken up.* – *If prompting is needed, read Scenario D in Appendix A (or another scenario as you see fit). Ask: Is this example relevant to USSPACECOM? How would those inside of USSPACECOM deal with this situation?* • *Facilitator will recap and prioritize problems that everyone seems to agree on.*	00:10 – 00:20
4.	**Question 2: Can you provide examples of discrimination, self-harm or suicide, sexual assault and sexual harassment, or hostile work environment in USSPACECOM? Please do not to use individual identifiers, and instead focus more on roles of those involved in response or the processes involved in addressing the situation.** • *Facilitator Notes: Ask participants to take a moment to write down some examples or, if they have none, to write "no comment" (wait 2 minutes). Have them fold their notes and collect them. Read and discuss the notes.* – *If prompting is needed, read Scenario C in Appendix A (or another scenario as you see fit). Ask: Is this example relevant to USSPACECOM? How would those inside of USSPACECOM deal with this situation?* – *Probes: Which DOD, command, and/or installation policies and reporting mechanisms are relevant to these problems? Do you believe there is consistent application of policies, reporting, and monitoring these problems?* • *Facilitator will recap opportunities everyone seems to agree on.*	00:20 – 00:30

5.	**Question 3: In what aspects of prevention and response to these workforce challenges does USSPACECOM bear responsibility versus the military services?**	00:30 – 00:45

	• *Facilitator Note: Listen. Solicit responses from participants who haven't spoken up*
	  – *If prompting is needed, read Scenario E in Appendix A (or another scenario as you see fit). Ask: Is this example relevant to USSPACECOM? How would those inside of USSPACECOM deal with this situation?*
	  – *Probe: Does this differ for civilian versus uniformed personnel?*
	
	• *Facilitator will recap elements of prevention and response for which USSPACECOM bears responsibility.*	

6.	**Question 4: What barriers exist to taking actions against discrimination, self-harm or suicide, sexual assault and sexual harassment, and hostile work environment?**	00:45 – 01:00

	• *Facilitator Note: Ensure discussion doesn't focus just on one barrier. Ensure barriers are connected to relevant actions.*
	  – *If prompting is needed, read Scenario E or B in Appendix. Ask: Is this example relevant to USSPACECOM? How would those inside of USSPACECOM deal with this situation? What barriers might present themselves?*
	  – *Probes: For individuals who experience a problematic behavior, what barriers exist to reporting, getting services, etc.? Is there effective communication of policies and procedures around these problems?*
	
	• *For command: What barriers exist to preventing and addressing these problems? Have you hired staff and allocated sufficient funding towards these efforts? Do any DOD or USSPACECOM policies/ reporting mechanisms create barriers to acting on these problems?*
	
	• *Facilitator will recap barriers and opportunities everyone seems to agree on.*	

7.	**Question 5: What are the levers your leadership at USSPACE-COM has the authority to pull that would improve the issues we discussed today?**	**01:00 – 01:15**
	• Facilitator Notes: It may be useful to note here that there may be policy levers that only OSD, or other higher headquarters, can pull. We would like to hear about what policy options are within USSPACECOM's control but also what is outside of their scope. Additionally, some policies may be left to the Services to address. We would like to hear what those are as well, but our main focus here is to identify the policy actions that USSPACECOM should pursue. *• Facilitator will recap available levers.*	
8.	**Question 6: Among those levers, what do you think USSPACE-COM should do to better address these issues?**	**01:15 – 01:25**
	• Facilitator Notes: We would like to hear which of the identified potential actions USSPACECOM should prioritize or focus on improving. *• Probe: How much do you self-identify with your Service (military only) and USSPACECOM? Would that change if these issues were addressed differently?* *• Facilitator will recap highest-priority levers.*	
9.	**Conclusion**	**01:25 – 01:30**
	• Thank you for your participation. Today's workshop is one out of several that we are holding this week. • We'll use the results from this workshop in a final report that is publicly available. • If you have any questions or concerns, please let us know offline now or in the future. – *Facilitator Note: Leave an additional 30 minutes for time should attendees want to continue the discussion. At this point, the facilitator should take a more passive role and observe the group dynamics. This part is not required.*	

Abbreviations

CAF	Comprehensive Airman Fitness
CCMD	combatant command
CCSA	Combatant Command Support Agent
DoD	U.S. Department of Defense
DoDI	Department of Defense Instruction
EAP	Employee Assistance Program
EEO	Equal Employment Opportunity
E-OSC	Expanded Operational Stress Control
IRC	Independent Review Commission
MEO	Military Equal Opportunity
OSD	Office of the Secretary of Defense
OUSD(P&R)	Office of the Under Secretary of Defense for Personnel and Readiness
R2	Ready and Resilient
SAPR	Sexual Assault Prevention and Response
SAPRO	Sexual Assault Prevention and Response Office
SHARP	Sexual Harassment and Assault Response and Prevention
TFF	Total Force Fitness
USSPACECOM	U.S. Space Command

References

Acosta, Joie D., Matthew Chinman, and Amy L. Shearer, *Countering Sexual Assault and Sexual Harassment in the U.S. Military: Lessons from RAND Research*, RAND Corporation, RR-A1318-1, 2021. As of November 20, 2023:
https://www.rand.org/pubs/research_reports/RRA1318-1.html

Air Force Instruction 90-5001, *Integrated Resilience*, U.S. Department of the Air Force, August 2, 2023.

American Psychological Association, "Resilience," webpage, undated. As of November 20, 2023:
https://www.apa.org/topics/resilience

Anderson, Lauren, Laura Campbell-Sills, Robert J. Ursano, Ronald C. Kessler, Xiaoying Sun, Steven G. Heeringa, Matthew K. Nock, Paul D. Bliese, Oscar I. Gonzalez, Gary H. Wynn, Sonia Jain, and Murray B. Stein, "Prospective Associations of Perceived Unit Cohesion with Postdeployment Mental Health Outcomes," *Depression and Anxiety*, Vol. 36, No. 6, June 2019.

Austin, Lloyd, "Immediate Actions to Counter Sexual Assault and Harassment and the Establishment of a 90-Day Independent Review Commission on Sexual Assault in the Military," memorandum for senior Pentagon leadership commanders of the combatant commands defense agency and DoD field activity directors, February 26, 2021.

Austin, Lloyd, "New DoD Actions to Prevent Suicide in the Military," memorandum for senior Pentagon leadership commanders of the combatant commands defense agency and DoD field activity directors, September 26, 2023.

"BLS Data Provides Further Evidence of Suicide Epidemic in Federal Agencies," *FEDagent*, January 9, 2020.

Bridges, Donna, Elizabeth Wulff, and Larissa Bamberry, "Resilience for Gender Inclusion: Developing a Model for Women in Male-Dominated Occupations," *Gender, Work and Organization*, Vol. 30, No. 1, January 2023.

Bur, Jessie, "DoD Has a Blind Spot for Civilian Employee Sexual Assaults," *Federal Times*, February 9, 2021.

Campbell-Sills, Laura, Xiaoying Sun, Ronald C. Kessler, Robert J. Ursano, Sonia Jain, and Murray B. Stein, "Exposure to Bullying or Hazing During Deployment and Mental Health Outcomes Among US Army Soldiers," *JAMA Network Open*, Vol. 6, No. 1, January 2023.

Centers for Disease Control and Prevention, "The Social-Ecological Model: A Framework for Prevention," webpage, last updated January 18, 2022. As of November 20, 2023:
https://www.cdc.gov/violenceprevention/about/social-ecologicalmodel.html

Centers for Disease Control and Prevention, National Center for Injury Prevention and Control, *STOP SV: A Technical Package to Prevent Sexual Violence*, 2016.

Chairman of the Joint Chiefs of Staff Instruction 3405.01, *Chairman's Total Force Fitness Framework*, September 23, 2013.

Chinman, Matthew, Patricia A. Ebener, Amy L. Shearer, Joie D. Acosta, and Sarah B. Hunter, *Getting to Outcomes© Operations Guide for U.S. Air Force Community Action Teams*, RAND Corporation, TL-311-AF, 2020. As of January 16, 2024:
https://www.rand.org/pubs/tools/TL311.html

Code of Federal Regulations, Title 29, Chapter XIV, Equal Employment Opportunity Commission.

Code of Federal Regulations, Title 29, Part 1604.11, Sexual Harassment.

Code of Federal Regulations, Title 32, Part 105.9, Commander and Management Procedures.

Cohen, Jacob, "A Coefficient of Agreement for Nominal Scales," *Educational and Psychological Measurement*, Vol. 20, No. 1, 1960.

Daniel, Samantha, Brice McKeever, Rachel Breslin, Rachel Clare, Ashlea Klahr, and Stephanie E. V. Brown, "Diversity, Equity, and Inclusion Correlates of Racial/Ethnic Harassment and Discrimination in the U.S. Military," *Military Psychology*, Vol. 35, No. 6, 2022.

Defense Health Agency, "Total Force Fitness (TFF): Program Update," presentation, U.S. Department of Defense, February 10, 2020.

Department of Defense Directive 5100.03, *Support of the Headquarters of Combatant and Subordinate Unified Commands*, incorporating change 1, U.S. Department of Defense, September 7, 2017.

Department of Defense Directive 6495.01, *Sexual Assault Prevention and Response (SAPR) Program*, incorporating change 5, U.S. Department of Defense, November 10, 2021.

Department of Defense Instruction 1020.03, *Harassment Prevention and Response in the Armed Forces*, Office of the Under Secretary of Defense for Personnel and Readiness, February 8, 2018.

Department of Defense Instruction 1350.02, *DoD Military Equal Opportunity Program*, incorporating change 1, Office of the Under Secretary of Defense for Personnel and Readiness, December 20, 2022.

Department of Defense Instruction 1400.25, *Civilian Personnel Management System: Awards*, Vol. 451, November 4, 2013.

Department of Defense Instruction 1438.06, *DoD Workplace Violence Prevention and Response Policy*, incorporating change 1, Office of the Under Secretary of Defense for Personnel and Readiness, May 4, 2020.

Department of Defense Instruction 6400.09, *DoD Policy on Integrated Primary Prevention of Self-Directed Harm and Prohibited Abuse or Harm*, Office of the Under Secretary of Defense for Personnel and Readiness, September 11, 2020.

Department of Defense Instruction 6400.11, *DoD Integrated Primary Prevention Policy for Prevention Workforce and Leaders*, Office of the Under Secretary of Defense for Personnel and Readiness, December 20, 2020.

Department of Defense Instruction 6490.16, *Defense Suicide Prevention Program*, incorporating change 3, Office of the Under Secretary of Defense for Personnel and Readiness, February 3, 2023.

Dickinson, James H., "Fiscal Year 2023 Priorities and Posture of United States Space Command," presentation to the U.S. Senate Armed Services Committee, March 1, 2022.

DoD—*See* U.S. Department of Defense.

DoD Directive—*See* Department of Defense Directive.

DoDI—*See* Department of Defense Instruction.

DoD, OUSD(P&R)—*See* U.S. Department of Defense, Office of the Under Secretary of Defense for Personnel and Readiness.

DoD, SAPRO—*See* U.S. Department of Defense, Sexual Assault Prevention and Response Office.

Executive Order 11246, As Amended, "Equal Employment Opportunity," Office of Federal Contract Compliance Programs, September 24, 1965.

Farmer, Carrie M., Katie Whipkey, and Margaret Chamberlin, *Programs Addressing Psychological Health and Resilience in the U.S. Department of Homeland Security*, RAND Corporation, RR-1952-DHS, 2019. As of November 20, 2023:
https://www.rand.org/pubs/research_reports/RR1952.html

Farris, Coreen, Terry L. Schell, Lisa H. Jaycox, and Robin L. Beckman, *Perceived Retaliation Against Military Sexual Assault Victims*, RAND Corporation, RR-2380-OSD, 2021. As of November 20, 2023:
https://www.rand.org/pubs/research_reports/RR2380.html

Farris, Coreen, Carra S. Sims, Terry L. Schell, Miriam Matthews, Sierra Smucker, Samantha Cohen, and Owen Hall, *Harassment and Discrimination on the Basis of Gender and Race/ Ethnicity in the FEMA Workforce*, RAND Corporation, RR-A383-1, 2020. As of November 20, 2023:
https://www.rand.org/pubs/research_reports/RRA383-1.html

Feijó, Fernando R., Débora D. Gräf, Neil Pearce, and Anaclaudia G. Fassa, "Risk Factors for Workplace Bullying: A Systematic Review," *International Journal of Environmental Research and Public Health*, Vol. 16, No. 11, May 2019.

Gedney, Christine R., David S. Wood, Brad Lundahl, and Robert P. Butters, "Sexual Assault Prevention Efforts in the U.S. Air Force: A Systematic Review and Content Analysis," *Journal of Interpersonal Violence,* Vol. 33, No. 3, February 2018.

Griffith, James, "The Sexual Harassment–Suicide Connection in the U.S. Military: Contextual Effects of Hostile Work Environment and Trusted Unit Leaders," *Suicide and Life-Threatening Behavior,* Vol. 49, No. 1, February 2019.

Hall, Kimberly Curry, Kirsten M. Keller, David Schulker, Sarah Weilant, Katherine L. Kidder, and Nelson Lim, *Improving Gender Diversity in the U.S. Coast Guard: Identifying Barriers to Female Retention*, RAND Corporation, RR-2770-DHS, 2019. As of November 20, 2023:
https://www.rand.org/pubs/research_reports/RR2770.html

Hamilton, Janette A., Jennifer A. Coleman, and William J. Davis, "Leadership Perspectives of Stigma-Related Barriers to Mental Health Care in the Military," *Military Behavioral Health*, Vol. 5, No. 1, 2017.

Harrell, Margaret C., and Laura L. Miller, *New Opportunities for Military Women: Effects Upon Readiness, Cohesion, and Morale*, RAND Corporation, MR-896-OSD, 1997. As of November 20, 2023:
https://www.rand.org/pubs/monograph_reports/MR896.html

Hepner, Kimberly A., Erika Litvin Bloom, Sydne Newberry, Jessica L. Sousa, Karen Chan Osilla, Marika Booth, Armenda Bialas, and Carolyn M. Rutter, "The Impact of Mindfulness Meditation Programs on Performance-Related Outcomes: Implications for the U.S. Army," *RAND Health Quarterly,* Vol. 10, No. 1, 2022. As of March 14, 2024:
https://www.rand.org/pubs/periodicals/health-quarterly/issues/v10/n1/09.html

Holland, Kathryn J., and Allison E. Cipriano, "Bystander Response to Sexual Assault Disclosures in the U.S. Military: Encouraging Survivors to Use Formal Resources," *American Journal of Community Psychology,* Vol. 64, Nos. 1–2, 2019.

Holliday, Stephanie Brooks, Sarah O. Meadows, Stephani L. Wrabel, Laura Werber, Christopher Joseph Doss, Wing Yi Chan, Lu Dong, and Brandon Crosby, *Assessing the Association Between Airmen Participation in Force Support Squadron Programs and Unit Cohesion: An Evaluation of the UNITE Initiative*, RAND Corporation, RR-A554-1, 2022. As of January 16, 2024: https://www.rand.org/pubs/research_reports/RRA554-1.html

Hom, Melanie A., Ian H. Stanley, Matthew E. Schneider, and Thomas E. Joiner, Jr., "A Systematic Review of Help-Seeking and Mental Health Service Utilization Among Military Service Members," *Clinical Psychology Review*, Vol. 53, 2017.

Hourani, Laurel L., Jason Williams, Pamela K. Lattimore, Jessica K. Morgan, Susan G. Hopkinson, Linda Jenkins, and Joel Cartwright, "Workplace Victimization Risk and Protective Factors for Suicidal Behavior Among Active Duty Military Personnel," *Journal of Affective Disorders,* Vol. 236, August 2018.

Johnson, Douglas C., Nathaniel J. Thom, Elizabeth A. Stanley, Lori Haase, Alan N. Simmons, Pei-An B. Shih, Wesley K. Thompson, Eric G. Potterat, Thomas R. Minor, and Martin P. Paulus, "Modifying Resilience Mechanisms in At-Risk Individuals: A Controlled Study of Mindfulness Training in Marines Preparing for Deployment," *American Journal of Psychiatry,* Vol. 171, No. 8, 2014.

Joint Base Elmendorf-Richardson, "Alaskan Command," webpage, undated. As of November 20, 2023: https://www.jber.jb.mil/Training-and-Airspace/Alaskan-Command

Joint Base San Antonio, "Resiliency," webpage, undated. As of November 20, 2023: https://www.jbsa.mil/Resources/Resiliency

Joint Knowledge Online, homepage, undated. As of March 4, 2024: https://jkodirect.jten.mil

Keller, Kirsten M., Miriam Matthews, Kimberly Curry Hall, and Melissa Bauman, *Hazing Prevention and Response: Training for Military Leaders*, RAND Corporation, TL-240-RC, 2017. As of February 27, 2024: https://www.rand.org/pubs/tools/TL240.html

Keller, Kirsten M., Miriam Matthews, Kimberly Curry Hall, William Marcellino, Jacqueline A. Mauro, and Nelson Lim, *Hazing in the U.S. Armed Forces: Recommendations for Hazing Prevention Policy and Practice*, RAND Corporation, RR-941-OSD, 2015. As of February 27, 2024: https://www.rand.org/pubs/research_reports/RR941.html

Kim, JaeYop, JoonBeom Kim, and SooKyung Park, "Military Hazing and Suicidal Ideation Among Active Duty Military Personnel: Serial Mediation Effects of Anger and Depressive Symptoms," *Journal of Affective Disorders,* Vol. 256, 2019.

Kim, Jae Yop, Joonbeom Kim, Sookyung Park, and Nicola Fear, "Workplace Victimization and Alcohol Misuse Among Junior Military Personnel: Mediating the Role of Anger," *Journal of Affective Disorders,* Vol. 294, 2021.

Klemmer, Cary Leonard, Ashley C. Schuyler, Mary Rose Mamey, Sheree M. Schrager, Carl Andrew Castro, Jeremy Goldbach, and Ian W. Holloway, "Health and Service-Related Impact of Sexual and Stalking Victimization During United States Military Service on LGBT Service Members," *Journal of Interpersonal Violence,* Vol. 37, Nos. 9–10, 2022.

Larsen, Sadie E., Christopher D. Nye, and Louise F. Fitzgerald, "Sexual Harassment Expanded: An Examination of the Relationships Among Sexual Harassment, Sex Discrimination, and Aggression in the Workplace," *Military Psychology,* Vol. 31, No. 1, 2019.

Larson, Kathlene, Nancy Grudens-Schuck, and Beverly Lundy Allen, "Can You Call It a Focus Group?" methodology brief, Iowa State University, May 2004.

Law, Charlie L., and Erica Harris, "Religious Discrimination and Accommodations in the U.S. Military: Best Practices for Leaders," *North American Journal of Psychology*, Vol. 21, No. 1, March 2019.

LeFeber, Tirzah Parrish, and Bernadette Solorzano, "Putting Suicide Policy Through the Wringer: Perspectives of Military Members Who Attempted to Kill Themselves," *International Journal of Environmental Research and Public Health*, Vol. 16, No. 21, November 2019.

Lopez, C. Todd, "Spacecom Built for Today's Strategic Environment," U.S. Department of Defense, September 27, 2019.

Low, Elizabeth C., Mario J. Scalora, Denise J. Bulling, Mark B. DeKraai, and Kyle R. Siddoway, "Willingness to Report in Military Workplace Violence Scenarios: Initial Findings from the Marine Corps on the Impact of Rank and Relationship to the Person of Concern," *Journal of Threat Assessment and Management*, Vol. 11, No. 1, 2024.

Maglione, Margaret A., Christine Chen, Armenda Bialas, Aneesa Motala, Joan Chang, Goke Akinniranye, and Susanne Hempel, *Stress Control for Military, Law Enforcement, and First Responders: A Systematic Review*, RAND Corporation, RR-A119-3, 2021. As of November 20, 2023:
https://www.rand.org/pubs/research_reports/RRA119-3.html

Marquis, Jefferson P., Coreen Farris, Kimberly Curry Hall, Kristy N. Kamarck, Nelson Lim, Douglas Shontz, Paul S. Steinberg, Robert Stewart, Thomas E. Trail, Jennie W. Wenger, Anny Wong, and Eunice C. Wong, *Improving Oversight and Coordination of Department of Defense Programs That Address Problematic Behaviors Among Military Personnel: Final Report*, RAND Corporation, RR-1352-OSD, 2017. As of November 20, 2023:
https://www.rand.org/pubs/research_reports/RR1352.html

Matthews, Miriam, and Coreen Farris, *Harmful Interpersonal Behaviors in the Department of the Air Force: Informing Prevention and Response*, RAND Corporation, PE-A908-1, April 2022. As of November 20, 2023:
https://www.rand.org/pubs/perspectives/PEA908-1.html

Matthews, Miriam, Coreen Farris, Terry L. Schell, and Kristie L. Gore, *Survey for Assessing Racial/Ethnic Harassment and Discrimination in the U.S. Military*, RAND Corporation, RR-A1246-2, 2021. As of November 20, 2023:
https://www.rand.org/pubs/research_reports/RRA1246-2.html

Matthews, Miriam, Coreen Farris, Margaret Tankard, and Michael Stephen Dunbar, *Needs of Male Sexual Assault Victims in the U.S. Armed Forces*, RAND Corporation, RR-2167-OSD, 2018. As of November 20, 2023:
https://www.rand.org/pubs/research_reports/RR2167.html

Matthews, Miriam, Kimberly Curry Hall, and Nelson Lim, *A Commander's Guide to Hazing Prevention*, RAND Corporation, TL-168-OSD, 2015. As of January 16, 2024:
https://www.rand.org/pubs/tools/TL168.html

Meadows, Sarah O., Stephanie Brooks Holliday, Wing Yi Chan, Stephani L. Wrabel, Margaret Tankard, Dana Schultz, Christopher M. Busque, Felix Knutson, Leslie Adrienne Payne, and Laura L. Miller, *Air Force Morale, Welfare, and Recreation Programs and Services: Contribution to Airman and Family Resilience and Readiness*, RAND Corporation, RR-2670-AF, 2019. As of November 20, 2023:
https://www.rand.org/pubs/research_reports/RR2670.html

Military OneSource, "2022 Demographics, Chapter 2: Active-Duty Members, Age," webpage, undated. As of January 18, 2024:
https://demographics.militaryonesource.mil/chapter-2-age

Miller, Laura L., Coreen Farris, Marek N. Posard, Miriam Matthews, Kirsten M. Keller, Sean Robson, Stephanie Brooks Holliday, Mauri Matsuda, Rachel M. Burns, Lisa Wagner, and Barbara Bicksler, *A Survey System to Assess Abuse and Misconduct Toward Air Force Students in Occupational Specialty Training*, RAND Corporation, RR-2692-AF, 2019. As of November 20, 2023:
https://www.rand.org/pubs/research_reports/RR2692.html

Morral, Andrew R., Miriam Matthews, Matthew Cefalu, Terry L. Schell, and Linda Cottrell, *Effects of Sexual Assault and Sexual Harassment on Separation from the U.S. Military: Findings from the 2014 RAND Military Workplace Study*, RAND Corporation, RR-870/10-OSD, 2021. As of November 20, 2023:
https://www.rand.org/pubs/research_reports/RR870z10.html

Nash, William P., and Patricia J. Watson, "Review of VA/DOD Clinical Practice Guideline on Management of Acute Stress and Interventions to Prevent Posttraumatic Stress Disorder," *Journal of Rehabilitation Research and Development*, Vol. 49, No. 5, 2012.

O'Keefe, Damian F., Leanne S. Son Hing, and Victor Catano, "Unethical Behaviour in the Military: The Role of Supervisor Ethicality, Ethical Climate, and Right-Wing Authoritarianism," *Military Psychology*, Vol. 35, No. 1, 2023.

Paparo, Samuel J., "Hazing," policy statement, U.S. Navy, July 15, 2021.

Potter, Sharyn J., and Jane G. Stapleton, "Translating Sexual Assault Prevention from a College Campus to a United States Military Installation: Piloting the Know-Your-Power Bystander Social Marketing Campaign," *Journal of Interpersonal Violence*, Vol. 27, No. 8, 2012.

RAND Corporation, *Actions the Army Can Take to Reduce Sexual Assault, Sexual Harassment, and Gender Discrimination*, RB-A1385-2, 2022. As of November 20, 2023:
https://www.rand.org/pubs/research_briefs/RBA1385-2.html

Robson, Sean, and Nicholas Salcedo, *Behavioral Fitness and Resilience: A Review of Relevant Constructs, Measures, and Links to Well-Being*, RAND Corporation, RR-103-AF, 2014. As of November 20, 2023:
https://www.rand.org/pubs/research_reports/RR103.html

Schooler, Carmi, "A Working Conceptualization of Social Structure: Mertonian Roots and Psychological and Sociocultural Relationships," *Social Psychology Quarterly*, Vol. 57, No. 3, September 1994.

South, Todd, "Early Data Shows 37% Suicide Decrease in Units with Holistic Health," *Army Times*, April 26, 2023.

Stander, Valerie A., and Cynthia J. Thomsen, "Sexual Harassment and Assault in the U.S. Military: A Review of Policy and Research Trends," *Military Medicine*, Vol. 181, Supp. 1, 2016.

Suicide Prevention and Response Independent Review Committee, *Preventing Suicide in the U.S. Military: Recommendations from the Suicide Prevention and Response Independent Review Committee*, U.S. Department of Defense, 2023.

Szayna, Thomas S., Eric V. Larson, Angela O'Mahony, Sean Robson, Agnes Gereben Schaefer, Miriam Matthews, J. Michael Polich, Lynsay Ayer, Derek Eaton, William Marcellino, Lisa Miyasho, Marek N. Posard, James Syme, Zev Winkelman, Cameron Wright, Megan Zander-Cotugno, and William Welser IV, *Considerations for Integrating Women into Closed Occupations in U.S. Special Operations Forces*, RAND Corporation, RR-1058-USSOCOM, 2015. As of November 20, 2023:
https://www.rand.org/pubs/research_reports/RR1058.html

U.S. Code, Title 10, Chapter 753, United States Military Academy; Section 7461, Policy on Sexual Harassment and Sexual Violence.

U.S. Code, Title 10, Chapter 953, United States Air Force Academy; Section 9461, Policy on Sexual Harassment and Sexual Violence.

U.S. Code, Title 10, Section 481, Racial and Ethnic Issues; Gender Issues: Surveys.

U.S. Code, Title 10, Section 481a, Workplace and Gender Relations Issues: Surveys of Department of Defense Civilian Employees.

U.S. Code, Title 10, Section 1074n, Annual Mental Health Assessments for Members of the Armed Forces.

U.S. Code, Title 10, Section 1090b, Commanding Officer and Supervisor Referrals of Members for Mental Health Evaluations.

U.S. Code, Title 10, Section 1561, Complaints of Sexual Harassment: Investigation by Commanding Officers.

U.S. Code, Title 10, Section 1562a, Complaints of Retaliation by Victims of Sexual Assault or Sexual Harassment and Related Persons: Tracking by Department of Defense.

U.S. Code, Title 10, Section 1565b, Victims of Sexual Assault: Access to Legal Assistance and Services of Sexual Assault Response Coordinators and Sexual Assault Victim Advocates.

U.S. Code, Title 10, Section 10219, Suicide Prevention and Resilience Program.

U.S. Department of Defense, *DoD Retaliation Prevention and Response Strategy: Regarding Sexual Assault and Harassment Reports*, April 2016.

U.S. Department of Defense, *Hard Truths and the Duty to Change: Recommendations from the Independent Review Commission on Sexual Assault in the Military*, July 2021.

U.S. Department of Defense, "DOD Announces New Actions to Prevent Suicide in the Military," press release, September 28, 2023.

U.S. Department of Defense, Office for Diversity, Equity, and Inclusion, homepage, undated. As of November 20, 2023:
https://diversity.defense.gov

U.S. Department of Defense, Office of People Analytics, *Department of Defense Civilian Employee Workplace and Gender Relations Report for Fiscal Year 2018: Biennial Report to Congress*, 2018.

U.S. Department of Defense, Office of People Analytics, *2017 Workplace and Equal Opportunity Survey of Active Duty Members: Executive Report*, August 2019.

U.S. Department of Defense, Office of People Analytics, *Unwanted Sexual Contact Reporting and Sexual Harassment Complaints in the Active Component: Findings from the 2021 Workplace and Gender Relations Survey of Military Members*, January 2023.

U.S. Department of Defense, Office of the Inspector General, *Evaluation of the Air Force Selection Process for the Permanent Location of the U.S. Space Command Headquarters*, May 2022.

U.S. Department of Defense, Office of the Under Secretary of Defense for Acquisition and Sustainment, *Department of Defense Climate Adaptation Plan*, September 2021.

U.S. Department of Defense, Office of the Under Secretary of Defense for Personnel and Readiness, *Annual Suicide Report: Calendar Year 2020*, September 2021.

U.S. Department of Defense, Office of the Under Secretary of Defense for Personnel and Readiness, *Prevention Plan of Action 2.0, 2022–2024*, May 2022.

U.S. Department of Defense, Sexual Assault Prevention and Response Office, "By Duty Status," webpage, undated. As of November 20, 2023:
https://sapr.mil/duty-status

U.S. Department of the Air Force, *Interpersonal Violence in the Department of the Air Force*, 2021.

U.S. Department of the Air Force, *The Joint Team*, September 2022.

U.S. Department of the Air Force Integrated Resilience, homepage, undated. As of November 20, 2023:
https://www.resilience.af.mil

USSPACECOM—*See* U.S. Space Command.

U.S. Space Command, "Equal Opportunity Coordinator," webpage, undated-a. As of November 20, 2023:
https://www.spacecom.mil/Support/Equal-Opportunity-Coordinator

U.S. Space Command, "Resilience Program," webpage, undated-b. As of December 7, 2023:
https://www.spacecom.mil/Support/Resilience-Program/

U.S. Space Command, "Sexual Assault Prevention and Response Victim Advocate," webpage, undated-c. As of January 16, 2024:
https://www.spacecom.mil/Support/Sexual-Assault-Prevention-and-Response-Victim-Advocate/

U.S. Space Command, *U.S. Space Command Human Capital Strategy 2023: Building Success Through Our Most Valuable Asset*, 2023a.

U.S. Space Command, "Resiliency Focus Week," presentation, August 2023b, Not available to the general public.

U.S. Space Command, "General Stephen N. Whiting," webpage, January 2024. As of January 18, 2024:
https://www.spacecom.mil/Leaders/Bio/Article/3640875/general-stephen-n-whiting/

U.S. Space Command Instruction 1101.01F, *Personnel Recognition Program*, U.S. Space Command, April 1, 2022.

Waldron, Jennifer J., "A Social Norms Approach to Hazing Prevention Workshops," *Journal of Sport Psychology in Action*, Vol. 3, No. 1, 2012.

Warlick, Craig A., Aaron Van Gorp, Nicole M. Farmer, Tristan Patterson, and Abigail Armstrong, "Comparing Burnout Between Graduate-Level and Professional Clinicians," *Training and Education in Professional Psychology*, Vol. 15, No. 2, 2021.

Zamorski, Mark A., "Suicide Prevention in Military Organizations," *International Review of Psychiatry*, Vol. 23, No. 2, 2011.